Cathedral Music Press Presents

Complete Book of Bach Chorales

edited by Jerry Silverman, M.A.

CONTENTS

INTRODUCTION

The analysis of these priceless musical gems, the chorales of Johann Sebastian Bach, represents a veritable "open sesame" into the world of harmony and voice leading to generations of music students. In a few short measures we are led through intertwining, often simple, yet always magnificent, expressions of faith through music and music through faith.

These chorales were, in effect, Bach's daily bread - freshly baked for each Sunday's service. The congregations that sang them probably knew all the melodies from long tradition, but they must have been continually amazed at the rich and varied settings that poured forth from the master's inexhaustable musical imagination.

Today's music students and congregations will certainly derive as much pleasure and inspiration from these chorales as Bach's contemporaries did. The purpose of this edition is to make the study and singing of the music and text as easy as possible by utilizing a large, clear format.

My first intense contact with the Bach chorales was in a year-long college theory course. Our textbook was the 1944 publication, *The 389 Chorales of Johann Sebastian Bach,* edited with English translations by choral conductor Henry S. Drinker. Drinker used as his source the 1898 Breitkopf and Härtel compilation, edited by Bernhard Richter. Drinker translated all the chorales into English. He then pasted gummed strips of paper over the German words and typed the English text onto the strips. The reproduction of this English edition was made by photo lithography and printed in a seven-by-ten inch page size. The end product of this admirable musicological endeavor was an invaluable volume of music whose lines of text are often hard to read because the reduced format necessitated a squeezing together of words and a general reduction of size.

Although this present edition of the complete chorales of J. S. Bach has availed itself of Drinker's translations, the music and the text have been entirely reset and printed in an easy-to-read, nine-by-twelve inch page size. It is hoped that this "user friendly" edition will inspire students and congregations to take a fresh look at this priceless musical treasure.

Jerry Silverman

****

In the Drinker edition the titles of the chorales and cantatas appear in German only. I have translated them into English. The references to B. A. (Bach Ausgabe/Bach Edition) are to the numbered volumes of the Bach Gesellschaft Edition which contain those chorales. The references in small type at the left, above the chorale, are to the composer or source of the melody; those under the chorale to the author of the text. The letters G. B., which appear occasionally after a composer or source, stand for Gesang Buch (Song Book).

Cathedral
MUSIC PRESS

Visit us on the Web at http://www.melbay.com — E-mail us at email@melbay.com

Index To English First Lines

Index To Original German First Lines
(Apostrophes at the ends of words are omitted)

Chorales Appropriate to Certain Occasions

1

Ach bleib bei uns, Herr Jesu Christ
Abide With Us, Lord Jesus Christ

B.A. 39, Nº 1

S. Calvisius, 1594

A - bide— with us, our Bless - ed Lord, as near - er draws—

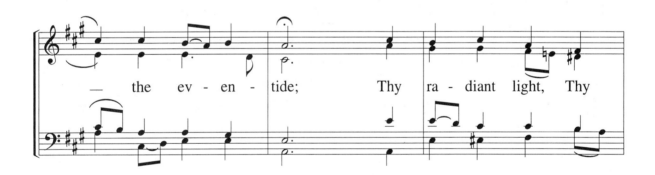

— the ev - en - tide; Thy ra - diant light, Thy

Ho - ly Word, Let ev - er still— with us— a - bide.

Nicolaus Selneccer, 1579

2

Ach Gott, erhör' mein Seufzen!
Oh God, Hear My Sighs!

B. A. 39, N° 2

Praxis pietatis, Frankfurt, 1662

Jac. Peter Schechs, 1648

3

Ach Gott und Herr
Oh God And Lord

B. A. 39, Nº 3

As hymnodus sacer; Leipzig, 1625

Ah God, my Lord, a heav-vy horde, the sins by me com-mit-ted! Thy Son a-lone can all a-tone, that I may be ac-quit-ted.

Martin Rutilius, 1604

4
Ach Gott und Herr
Oh God And Lord

Cantata 48. Ich elender Mensch
I Wretched Man

B. A. 10 S, 288

As hymnodus sacer; Leipzig, 1625

On earth be - low dis - tress and woe must fol - low our trans -
gres - sion, that we a - bove may gain— Thy love through
Je - sus' in - ter - ces - sion.

Martin Rutilius, 1604

5

Ach Gott, vom Himmel sieh' darein
O God, From Heaven, Do Look Down

Cantata 153. Schau lieber Gott, wie meine Feind'

See, Dear God, How Mine Enemies

B. A. 32, 43

Erfurter Enchiridion, 1524

See, dear - est God, the ma - ny foes, that
foul - ly deal such might - y blows, that

con - stant - ly as - sail me, So fail me. The
strength I fear will

world, the de - vil and the flesh my fee - ble soul would

soon en - mesh, did not Thy Grace a - vail me.

Dav. Denicke, 1661

17

6
Ach Gott, vom Himmel sieh' darein
O God, From Heaven, Do Look Down

Cant. 77. Du sollst Gott, deinen Herren, lieben.

Thou Shallt Love God, Thy Lord

Erfurter Enchiridion, 1524   B.A. 18, 254

Thou, Je-sus, who art far a-bove all oth-ers as love's teach-er, Give me, too, grace and strength to love my God and fel-low crea-ture; That I may do what-e'er I can, in friend-ship true for ev-'ry man, ac-cord-ing to Thy plea-sure.

7
Ach Gott, vom Himmel sieh' darein
O God, From Heaven, Do Look Down

Cantata 2. Ach Gott, vom Himmel sieh' darein
O God, From Heaven, Do Look Down

B. A. 1, 72

Erfurter Enchiridion, 1534

Ah God from Hea - ven, look a-new; may we Thy pi - ty
scan - ty are Thy Faith - ful Few, let us not be for-
Do Thou, dear God, be - side us stand, for rogues are all a-
guard us with Thy migh - ty hand from foes who seek to

1. & 3.
wa - ken. How
bout us. And

2. & 4.
sa - ken. Thy Ho - ly Word men
flout us. The god - less rab - ble

hold not true, nor seek with Faith, Thy will to do; Thy
'round we see, where right - eous Chris - tian folk should be; Lord,

Folk are sore - ly sha - ken.
let them ne - ver rout us!

Martin Luther, 1524

8
Ach Gott, wie manches Herzeleid
(Herr Jesu Christ, mein's Lebens Licht)

O God, How Much Heartache
(Lord Jesus Christ, Light Of My Life)

Cantata 3. Ach Gott, wie manches Herzeleid

O God, How Much Heartache

B. A. 1, 94

As hymnodus sacer, Leipzig 1625

Jos. Clauder, 1630

Ah. God, how sad and sick at heart am
Sus - tain my heart by Faith di - vine, that

I in this un - hap - py time. The nar - row path is
I in life and death be Thine. I pray Thee hark - en,

full of woe, by which to Heav - en I must climb.
Lord, to me; My Sa - viour, would I were with Thee

Mart Moller ? 1590

9
Ach Gott, wie manches Herzeleid
(Herr Jesu Christ, mein's Herzeleid)
O God, How Much Heartache
(Lord Jesus Christ, Light Of My Life)

Cantata 153. Schau, lieber Gott!

Look, Dear God!

B. A. 32, 58

As hymodus sacer, Leipzig, 1625

Jos. Clauder, 1630

Lord, here on earth, my soul__ pre - pare,
Hold my en - dea - vor broad__ and high;
Strength-en my faith,__ from doubt - ing free;

pa - tient and glad, my Cross to bear.
let me ful - fill it ere I die.
liv - ing and dy - ing all for Thee.

Fill me with faith and hope and love,
Help me my way - ward flesh to tame;
Je - sus my com - fort, hear my prayer:

rea - dy to serve Thee there a - bove.
Keep Thou me free from sin and shame.
"Sa - viour, would I were with Thee There."

Martin Moller, 1587

10

Ach, was soll ich Sünder machen
O, What Shall I, Sinner, Do

B. A. 39, Nº 7

Joh. Flitner, 1661

How may I, in sin for - sa - ken, my re - pen - tance now be - gin? Con - sience loud pro - claims my sin; yet my soul be - gins to wa - ken! This, the trust to which I cleave; Je - sus I will nev - er leave.

Martin Moller, 1661

11

Ach wie flüchtig, ach wie nichtig
Ah How Fleeting, Ah How Futile

Cantata 26. Ach wie flüchtig

Ah How Fleeting

B.A. 5, I, 26

Michael Franck, 1652

Ah how fleet-ing, ah how fu - tile is a man's ex - ist - ence!
Ah how fleet-ing, ah how fu - tile is a man's en - dea - vor!

As a cloud - let, quick ap - pear - ing, van - ish - es when
All the works by man cre - at - ed, van - ish and are

skies are clear - ing, so our lives, for death is near - ing.
dis - si - pat - ed. Trust in God and live for - ev - er.

Michael Franck, 1652

23

12

Allein Gott in der Höh' sei Ehr'
To God On High Alone Be Praise

B. A. 39, N° 8

Valentin Schumannsches G. B. 1539 (1526)

To— God on high a - lone be praise and
by, through all our mor - tal days, no

thanks that— he— doth bless— us, Where -
ev - il— will— dis-

tress— us. For

God de - lights to grant— us peace. He bids that feuds and

strife shall cease, and wars no more— op - press— us.

Nic. Decius, 1526

24

13
Allein Gott in der Höh' sei Ehr'
To God On High Alone Be Praise

Cantata 104. Du Hirte Israel, höre

Thou Shepherd Israel, Listen

B. A. 23, 116

Nic. Decius, 1526
Valentin Schumannsches G. B., 1539

The— Lord my Faith - ful Shep - herd is, my
mea - dows deep He guides His sheep, in

ev - 'ry— want— sup ply - ing. Through
ver - dant— val - leys ly - ing. By

wa - ters still He lead - eth me, in pas - tures green He

feed - eth me, and so my soul— re - stor - eth.

Cornelius Becker, 1602

25

14
Allein Gott in der Höh' sei Ehr'
To God On High Alone Be Praise

Cantata 112. Der Herr ist mein getreuer Hirt
The Lord Is My Faithful Shepherd

Nic. Decius, 1526

Valentin Schumannsches G. B., 1539   B. A. 24, 48

The— Lord, my God, my Shep - herd is, for
sa - tis - fi - eth all my wants, nor
And— so through all my mor - tal days, shall
I will dwell and sing Thy praise with -

me He ev - er car - eth. He spar - eth. By
a - ny bless - ing
good - ness fail me nev - er. And ev - er. On
in Thy house for

wa - ters still He lead - eth me, In pas - tures green He
earth, mid good - ly folk se - cure, And af - ter death, sal -

feed - eth me, and so my soul re - stor - eth.
va - tion sure, through Je - sus Christ, the Sa - viour.

Wolfgang Musculus ? 1531 and 1533

26

15
Allein zu dir, Herr Jesu Christ
In Thee Alone, Lord Jesus Christ

Val. Babst, 1545

B.A. 39, Nº 9

In Thee a - lone,— Lord Je - sus Christ, I
Thee my— Hope— and Trust— and Guide, I

place my firm re - li - ance. With
bid the world de - fi - ance.

ance. On earth there has been born no man, no mor - tal found since

time be - gan, who in my need can suc - cor me. I cry—

— to Thee, that Thou my Help— and Com - fort be.

Jöh. Schneesing, 1542

16
Allein zu dir, Herr Jesu Christ
To Thee Alone, Lord Jesus Christ

Cantata 33. Allein zu dir, Herr Jesu Christ

To Thee Alone, Lord Jesus Christ

B. A. 7, 114

Val. Babst G.B. 1543

All praise to God enthroned on high, from
well-loved Son we glorify, 'tis

Whom no pow'r can serve us. His
He Who will pre- serve us. All

hon-or to the Ho-ly Ghost, Who helps us when we need help most. For fa-vor in Their

eyes we pray, On earth here to-day and ev-er af-ter-ward al-way.

Jöh. Schneesing, 1542

17
Alle Menschen müssen sterben
Every Mortal Soon Must Perish

B. A. 39, N° 10

Joh. Hintze, 1678

Ev - 'ry mor - tal soon must per - ish, ev - 'ry liv - ing
Like the grass must fade and with - er, and a - gain be

crea - ture too.
born a - new. Mor - tal flesh to dust re - turn ing,

life e - ter - nal thus is earn - ing. There the faith - ful

souls will see God's tran - scen - dent ma - jes - ty.

Johann Georg Albinus, 1652 (Joh. Rosemüller?)

18
Alle Menschen müssen sterben
Every Mortal Soon Must Perish

Cantata 162. Ach, ich sehe, jetzt da ich zur Hochzeit gehe

Ah, I See, Now I Am Going To The Wedding

B.A. 33, 46

Taken from the melody "Jesu, der du meine Seele"
("Jesus, Thou My Soul") Variant by Bach (?)

Johann Georg Albinius, 1652 (Joh. Rosenmüller?)

30

19
Alles ist an Gottes Segen
Everything Comes From God's Blessing

B. A. 39, N° 11

From J. B. König's Chorale Book, 1738 (variant)

More than all we are pos - sess - ing is the Fa - ther's

pre - cious bless - ing, bet - ter far— than— goods and gold.

He who trusts in God's sal - va tion, knows no fear or

tre - pi da - tion; Strong is he,— se - rene and— bold.

1676

20

Als der gütige Gott
When The Benevolent God

B. A. 39, N° 12

Mich. Weisse, 1531
Joh. Crüger, 1640

That God at last might do the work that he had
To Na-za-reth came he, a Vir-gin there to

planned, His an-gel quick-ly flew to Ga-li-le-a
tell; To Ma-ry, name a-dored, that she would one day

Land; His name was Ga-bri-el.
be the mo-ther of Our Lord.

Mich. Weisse, 1531

21

Als Jesus Christus in der Nacht
When Jesus Christ At Night

B. A. 39, N° 13

Joh. Crüger, 1649

The night our Sa - viour was be - trayed, be -
There in His hands he took the bread and
"Take this and eat, for this is I, my

fore His tri - bu - la - tion, A so - lemn sac - ra -
broke it with his fin - gers, Gave thanks to God on
bo - dy for you bro - ken. My pre - scence this will

ment He made to com - pass our sal - va - tion.
High, and said, to His dis - ci - ples speak - ing:
tes - ti - fy for - ev - er as a To - ken."

Joh. Heermann, 1636

22

Als vierzig Tag' nach Ostern war'n
(Erschienen ist der herrlich' Tag)

Full Forty Days Past Easter Day
(The Glorious Day Shines Forth)

B. A. 39, N° 14

Nic. Heerman, 1560 (quite transformed)

Full for-ty days past Eas - ter Day, Christ's work was done, He must a-way. With His dis-ciples stand-ing by, stand-ing by, from off the Mount He rose on High. Hal-le-lu-jah!

Nic. Heermann, 1560

23
An Wasserflüssen Babylon
Beside The Streams Of Babylon

B. A. 39, N° 15

Wolfgang Dachstein, 1525

Be - side the streams of Ba - by - lon, our wea - ry vi - gil
we re - mem - ber Zi - on yon, we ne - ver cease from

keep - ing. When weep - ing. We hang our harps, in our de - spair, up -

on the weep ing wil - lows there, and mourn our de - gra - da - tion. All

we hold dear our foes de - fame, and we must suf - fer

slur and shame in dai - ly tri - bu - la - tion.

tri - bu - la - tion.

Wolfgang Dachstein, 1525

24

Auf, auf, mein Herz, und du mein ganzer Sinn
Up, Up, My Heart, And You My Mortal Mind

B. A. 39, N° 16

Stenger, 1663

Up, up, my heart, and thou my mor - tal mind; leave things of earth and world - ly work be - hind. If thou wouldst gain to__ God and His sal - va - tion, from bo - dy's pri - son seek thou li - ber - a - tion.

Martin Opitz, 1624

25

Auf meinem lieben Gott
On My Beloved God

Cantata 188. Ich habe meine Zuversicht

I Have My Trust

B. A. 37, 212

J. H. Schein, 1627

Be lov - ed God will heed my cry to Him in need. My hope and my sal - va - tion from trial and tri - bu - la - tion. From ev - il He pro - tects me; in all my ways di - rects me.

Siegmund Weingärtner, 1609

26
Auf meinen lieben Gott
On My Beloved God

Cantata 89. Was soll ich aus dir machen,Ephraim?

What Shall I make Of Thee, Ephraim?

B. A. 20, 212

J. H. Schein, 1627

Ah, whi - ther may I fly? So sore dis - tressed am
How - ev - er sore my need, my Lord will ev - er

I. Where leav - ing sin be - hind me, may
heed. I look for my sal - va - tion, to

I de - liv - 'rance find me? Though ev - 'ry one con -
Je - sus' tri - bu - la - tion, where - by I tri - umph

dole me, the world can - not con - sole me.
glo - rious, o'er Hell and sin vic - to - rious.

Johann Heermann, 1630

38

27
Auf meinem lieben Gott
On My Beloved God

Cantata 136. Erforsche mich, Gott

Search Me, God

B.A. 28, 164

J. H. Schein, 1627

Thy blood, e - lix - ir pure, con - tains a po - tion sure to cleanse, though Sa - tan ra - ges, the sins of all the a - ges. Re - leased from sin's sub - jec - tion, we live by Thy di - rec - tion.

Johann Heermann, 1630

28

Auf meinen lieben Gott
On My Beloved God

Cantata 5. Wo soll ich fliehen hin?
Whither Shall I Flee?

B. A. 1, 150

J. H. Schein, 1637

Lead Thou my heart and will, Thy bid - ding to ful -
fill, And grant that no - thing ev - er shall
me from Thee dis - sev - er; in love for - ev - er
plight - ed, with Thee as one u - nit - ed.

Joh. Heermann, 1630

29

Auf meinen lieben Gott
On My Beloved God

Cant. 148. Bringet dem Herrn ehre seines Namens

Bring Honor Unto The Name Of The Lord

B. A. 1, 150

J. H. Schein, 1637

Lead Thou my heart and will Thy bid - ding to ful -

fil. and grant that no - thing ev - er shall

me from Thee dis - se - ver; In love for - ev - er

plight - ed with Thee as one u - nit - ed.

Joh. Heermann, 1630

30
Aus meines Herzens Grunde
From The Bottom Of My Heart

B. A. 39, N ° 17

Dav. Wolder, 1598

From out my heart I praise Thee, this
give my Thee thanks both here to - day, and

morn - ing with my song, And long. O God,— from
all my whole life

ev - 'ry - one to Thee en - throned, by glo -

ry, through Je - sus Christ our Sa -

viour, Thine own be - got - ten Son.

First publication, 1592

31

Aus tiefer Noth schrei ich zu dir
In Deep Despair I Cry To Thee

Cantata 38. Aus tiefer Noth schrei ich zu dir.

In Deep Despair I Cry To Thee

B. A. 7, 300

Martin Luther, 1524

Martin Luther, 1524

32

Befiehl du deine Wege
Entrust Thy Ways

B. A. 39, N° 20

Barth. Gesius, 1603

En - | trust thy ways un - | to Him, and | all thy spi - rit
ev - er faith ful | Guar - dian who | guides the winds and

craves; The_ | waves, Who_ | rules the clouds_ of | Hea - ven, and

bids the breez - es | blow, | He_ best can choose the

path - way, on | which our steps should | go.

P. Gerhardt, 1658

33

Christ, der du bist der helle Tag
Christ, Who Art The Light Of Day
Christe, qui lux es et dies

B. A. 39, N° 21

G. B. of the Böhm brothers, 1586

O Christ, who art the Light of Day, be-fore which night must needs give way; Thou shin-est down from Heav-en's height, and art the Preach-er of the Light; Thou art the Preach-er of the Light.

Erasmus Albertus, 1556

34

Christe, der du bist Tag und Licht
Christ, Who Art Day And Night

B. A. 39, N° 22

Jos. Klug G. B. 1535

O Christ, who art the Light of Day, naught
We ask of Thee Thy godly might to

may we hide from Thee a - way. Thou
guard us, Lord, through - out the night. Pro -

Bea - con of the Fa - ther's light, teach
tect, us, Lord, from all dis - tress, God,

us the way of Truth and Right.
Fa - ther Thou of Kind - li - ness.

Wolfg. Meuslin, 1526

35

Christe, du Beistand deiner Kreuzgemeinde
Christ, Thou Counsel Of Your Cross-Congregation

B. A. 39, N° 23

Matthäus Apelles von Löwenstern, 1644

O Christ, pro-tect us; us thy faith-ful_ ser - vants; come help us now, we pray Thee, Lord, our Sa - viour. Rout Thou the foe - men who so fierce sur - round us; lest they con-found us, lest they con-found us.

Matthäus Apelles von Löwenstern, 1644

36

Christ ist erstanden
Christ Is Risen

B. A. 39, N° 24

Jos. Klug, 1535   Translation by Bishop Myles Cloverdale, 1539

Christ is now rys'n a - gayne from His death and all His payne. There - for - e wyll we mer - ry be, and wyll re - joyse with Hym glad - ly. Ki - ri el - ey - son. Had He not rys - en a - gayne, we had ben lost, this is playne. But sen He is rys -

Already known around 1200

en in dede, let us love Hym all with spede.

Ki - ri el - ey - son. Al -

le - lu - ja, al - le - lu - ja, al - le lu - ja! Ther -

fore glad now wyll we be, and re - joyse in

Hym one - ly. Ki - ri el - ey - son.

37

Christ ist erstanden
Christ Is Risen

Cantata 66. Erfreut euch, ihr Herzen

Rejoice, Ye Hearts

B. A. 16, 214

Jos. Klug G. B. 1535

Al - le - lu - ja, al - le - lu - ja, al - le - lu - ja! So

let us all now joy - ful be, and trust in God, in

Ky - ri - e ———

Him on - ly! Ky - ri - e e - leis!

Known around 1200

38

Christ lag in Todesbanded
Christ Lay By Death Enshrouded

B. A. 39, N° 25

Joh. Walther G. B. 1524

Christ lay by death en - shroud - ed, from mor - tal sins to save us. He gave us. So now let us joy - ful be, and mag - ni - fy Him thank - ful - ly. And sing we Al - le - lu - ja, al - le - lu - jah!

is a - gain a - ri - sen, e - ter - nal life He

Martin Luther, 1524

39

Christ lag in Todesbanden
Christ Lay By Death Enshrouded

B. A. 39, N° 26

Joh. Walther G. B. 1524

Martin Luther, 1523

40

Christ lag in Todesbanden
Christ Lay By Death Enshrouded

Cantata 158. Der Friede sei mit dir   May Peace Be With You

B. A. 32, 154

Joh. Walther, 1524

The Eas-ter Lamb for us was slain, God's prom-ised boon be-
hung He there up - on the Cross, with Love Su - per - nal

stow - ing. High
glow - ing.

His Blood, sprin - kled

on our door, with Faith, bade Death to pass us o'er; The

Upper version: 1786 Edition;   Lower version: Cantata 158.

Slay-er can - not harm us. Hal - le - lu - ja.

Hal - le-lu - ja.

M. Luther, 1524

41

Christ lag in Todesbanden
Christ Lay By Death Enshrouded

Cantata 4. Christ lag in Todesbanden 1, 124

Joh. Walther G. B. 1524

We ce - le - brate this Ho - ly Feast, in re - ver - ence u -
ev - il_ lea - ven works no more, Thy Word its curse has_

nit - ed. The right - ed. Christ's_own self the_ feast will be, and

nou - rish our_ souls that we by Faith may_ gain sal -

va - tion. Hal - le - le - lu - ja.

Martin Luther, 1524

54

42

Christum wir sollen loben schon
We Should Praise Christ Willingly

Cantata 121. Christum wir sollen loben schon
We Should Praise Christ Willingly

Erfurt, 1524

B. A. 26, 20

In thank-ful praise sing ev-'ry-one to Christ, the Vir-gin Ma-ry's Son. With praise a-dore the Ho-ly Three, hence-forth for all E-ter-ni-ty.

Martin Luther, 1524

55

43

Christ, unser Herr, zum Jordan kam
Christ, Our Lord, Came To The Jordan

B. A. 39, N° 27

Joh. Walther, 1524

To— Jor - dan stream came Christ, our— Lord, Saint John be - side Him
tised Him there in Jor - dan's— ford at Might - y God's com -

stand - ing, Bap - mand - ing. He thus pre-pared for us a bath in

which to drown— death's ter - ror; To wash a - way all sin— and wrath, ef -

face for each— his er - ror, and fire a - new our cour - age.

Martin Luther, 1541

44

Christ, unser Herr, zum Jordan kam
Christ, Our Lord, Came To Jordan

Cantata 7. Christ, unser Herr, zum Jordan kam
Christ, Our Lord, Came To The Jordan

B. A. 1, 210

Joh. Walther G. B. 1524

Martin Luther, 1541

45

Christ, unser Herr, zum Jordan kam
Christ, Our Lord, Came to The Jordan

Cantata 176. Es ist ein trotzig und versagt Ding

It Is An Insolent And Discouraging Affair

B.A. 35, 198

Joh. Walther G. B., 1524

Paul Gerhardt, 1656

46

Christus, der ist mein Leben
Christ, He Is My Life

B. A. 39, N° 28

Melchior Vulpius, 1609

For Christ, my Sa - viour, live I, so

death for me is gain. My all to Je - sus

give I, and joy su - preme at - tain.

Melchior Vulpius G. B. 1609

47

Christus, der ist mein Leben
Christ, He Is My Life

B. A. 39, N° 29

Melchior Vulpius, 1609

For Christ, my Sa - viour, live I, dy dy dy - - dy - ing ing ing - ing glo - ry I gain. My all to Je - sus give I, and joy su - preme at - tain.

Melchior Vulpius, 1609

60

48
Christus, der uns selig macht
Christ, Who Makes Us Happy

B. A. 39, N° 30

Mich. Weisse, 1531

Christ, who knew no sin or wrong, like a thief was ta - ken.

Led be - fore a god - less throng, by His friends for - sa - ken.

He, who our sal - va - tion won, false - ly was con -

vic - ted; scoffed at scorned and spat up -

pre - dic - ted.

on, as the Word pre - dic - ted.

Word pre - dic ted

Mich. Weisse. 1531

pre - dic - ted.

49

Christus, der uns selig macht
Christ, Who Makes Us Happy

Johannes-Passion

St. John Passion

B. A. 12, I, 43

Mich Weisse, 1531

Christ, who knew no sin or wrong, like a thief was ta - ken.

Led be - fore a god - less throng, by his friends for - sa - ken.

He, who our sal - va - tion won, false - ly was con - vic - ted;

pre - dic - ted.

Scoffed at scorned and spat up - on, as the Word pre - dic - ted.

dic - ted.

Mich. Weisse, 1531

50
Christus, der uns selig macht
Christ, Who Makes Us Happy

Johannes-Passion
St. John Passion

B. A. 12, I, 121

Mich Weisse, 1531

Help, O Christ, that through the pain, Thou hast suf-fered for__ us,

Sin and vice we may__ dis-dain, ev - il ways ab - hor__ us.

On Thy death and why Thou__ died, we must pon-der du - ly;

tru - ly.

We, tho' weak,__ have right - ly tried, Lord, to thank Thee tru - ly.

tru - ly.

Mich. Weisse, 531

51

Christus ist ersanden, hat überwunden
Christ Is Risen, He Has Over come

B. A. 39, N° 31

Mich. Weisse, 1531

Mich. Weisse, 1531

Da der Herr Christ zu Tische sass
When Lord Christ Sat At The Table

B. A. 39, N° 32

Görlitz G. B. 1611

Nic. Herman, 1358

53

Danket dem Herren, denn er ist sehr freundlich
Thank The Lord, For He Is Very Friendly

B. A. 39, N° 33

Senfl (tenor melody), 1534

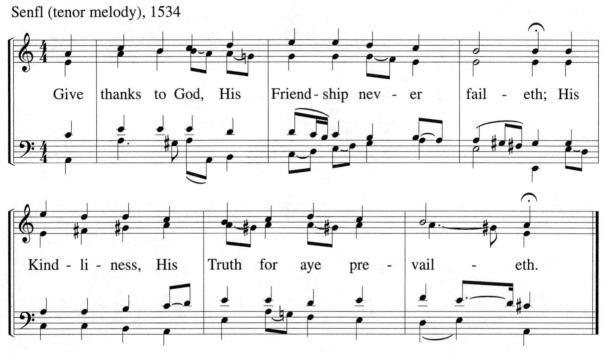

Give thanks to God, His Friend-ship nev - er fail - eth; His Kind - li - ness, His Truth for aye pre - vail - eth.

Joh. Horn, 1544

54

Thanked Be God On High
Dank sei Gott in der Höhe

B. A. 39, N° 34

Barth. Gesius, 1605

I thank my God in Hea - ven, as dawns an - oth - er
I from sleep have ris - en, re - freshed and strong and

day, That gay. The night was dark a - round me, but

well_ Thou guard - ed me; that safe the morn - ing

found me, I owe, my God, to Thee.

Joh. Mühlmann, 1618

55

Das alte Jahr vergangen ist
The Old Year Is Past

B. A. 39, N° 35

Joh. Steurlein, 1588

The year is— past and well may we, to Thee, Lord— Je - sus,

thank - ful be, that Thou from dan - gers,— doubts and fears, hast

guard - ed us through all— these years; From ev - il, dan - gers,

doubts and fears, hast guard - ed us through all these years.

Joh. Steurlein ? 1588

56

Das alte Jahr vergangen ist
The Old Year Is Past

B. A. 39, N° 36

Joh. Steurlein, 1588

The year is— past and well— may we, to Thee, Lord— Je - sus, thank - ful be, that Thou, from dan - gers,— doubts and fears, hast guard - ed us through all— these years; From ev - il, dan - gers, doubts and fears, hast guard - ed us through all these years.

Joh. Steurlein ? 1588

57

Das neugeborne Kindelein
The New-Born Little Child

Cantata 122. Das neugeborne Kindelein
The New-Born Little Child

B. A. 26, 40

Melch. Vulpius, 1609

Un - to the world＿ this hap - py morn,
Sing out, ye voi - ces, loud＿ and clear,

our lit - tle Je - sus Child was born.
Je - sus has end - ed all our fear;

Christ - ians re - joice,＿ the news＿ to hear,
Sing out, ye voi - ces, high＿ and low,

prom - is - ing all＿ a glad＿ New Year.
Je - sus has end - ed all＿ our woe.

Cyriacus Schneegass, 1597

58

Das walt' Gott Vater und Gott Sohn
May God The Father And God The Son Grant It

B. A. 39, N° 37

Dan Vetter, 1713

Thou God the Fa - ther, God the Son, Thou
Ho - ly Ghost, Thy will be done. In ear - ly dawn we
come to pray, and wor - ship Thee, as breaks the day.

Mart. Böhm, 1608

59

Das walt' mein Gott
Grant It, My God

Gotha, Cantionale 1648
Vopelius, 1682

B. A. 39, N° 38

As willed the Three: Fa - ther, Son and
My ev - 'ry step in the name of

Ho - ly Ghost, They have cre - at - ed me. My
God I take, Send Thou Thy help to me. Come

bo - dy, they al - lowed me, With soul and life en -
ear - ly, Lord, to meet me, With Grace and Bless - ing

dowed me, in like - ness, Lord, to Thee.
greet me, de - ny not Thou my plea.

Bas. Förtsch ? 1613

60

Den Vater dort oben
To The Father There On High

B. A. 39, N° 39

Mich. Weisse, 1531

To the Fa - ther, prai - ses, all Cre - a - tion rai - ses.

Kind - ly He us all has fed, giv - en us our dai - ly bread.

Praise to Je - sus Christ, His Son; Him Who our sal -

va - tion won, high in Heav'n en - thron - ed.

Mich. Weisse, 1531

61

Der du bist drei in Einigkeit
You Who Are Three In Unity

B. A. 39, N° 40

J. Herm. Schein, 1627

Thou ve - ry God, the Three in One, art God ere time was yet be - gun, When sun is set and it is night, let shine for us Thy Ho - ly light.

Martin Luther, 1543

62

Der Tag, der ist so freudenreich
The Day That Is So Rich In Joy

J. Klug G. B. 1535

B. A. 39, N° 41

Old Christmas song: Dies est lætitiae

63

Des heil'gen Geistes reiche Gnad'
The Holy Ghost's Rich Grace

B. A. 39, N° 42

J. Herm. Schein, 1627

Grace by the Ho - ly Ghost be - stowed!

Tongues as of fire a - bout them glowed! A
a - bout them

mi - ra - cle did then be - fall.
did then

Spake they with tongues strange to them all.
strange strange to

Arrangement of the hymn: Spiritus sancti gratia

64

Die Nacht ist kommen
The Night Is Falling

G. B. of the Böhm brothers, 1586
J. H. Schein, 1627

B. A. 39, N° 43

The night is fall - ing, now we all in sleep

rest; God or - ders_ all things, as He con - si - ders

best, while we are sleep - ing, by His pro - tec - tion

blest, and in His keep - ing.

Peter Herbert, 1630

65

Die Sonn' hat sich mit ihrem Glanz
The Sun Has With Its Brightness

B. A. 39, N° 44

French Psalms, Geneva, 1542

The day is done, the sun a-gain de - scend - ing; the
toil of man an - oth - er day is end - ing. The dark-ning night bids
bird to seek his nest, calls man and beast and all the world to rest.

Josua Stegmann, 1630

66

Dies sind die heil'gen zehn Gebot
These Are The Holy Ten Commandments

B. A. 39, N° 45

Erfurt, 1524

On Si - nai Moun-tain Mo - ses trod, and there re - ceived from

Migh - ty God the Ten Com - mand-ments, gra - ven deep, which

God, his Lord, bade him keep. Ky - rie E - leis'.

Martin Luther, 1524

67

Dir, dir Jehova, will ich singen
To Thou, Jehova, Will I Sing

B. A. 39, N° 45

J. S. Bach, 1725

To Thee,_____ Je - ho - va, come_____ I
Thee_____ my__ mu - sic come_____ I

sing - ing; where is an - oth - er__ God__ like un - to
bring - ing; make Thou my mel - o - dies__ stur - dy and

Thee? To free? In Je - sus' Name do__ I__

ten - der them here, so may they_____

sound de - light - ful to Thine___ ear.

Bath. Crasselius, 1697

68

Du Friedenfürst, Herr Jesu Christ
Thou Prince Of Peace, Lord Jesus Christ

Cantata 67, Halt im Gedächtniss Jesum Christ

Keep Jesus In Your Thoughts

B. A. 16, 246

Barth Gesius, 1601

Thou Prince of Peace, to Thee we bow, Lord Je-sus, God and
life and death the Help-er Thou, of all Thy faith-ful
man. In clan. So now we all in Thy Name call, and
ask Thy Fa - ther's bless - ing.

Jacob Ebert, 1601

69

Du Friedefürst, Herr Jesu Christ
Thou Prince Of Peace, Lord Jesus Christ

Cantata 116, Du Friedefürst

Thou Prince Of Peace

Barth Gesius, 1601   B. A.24, 156

En- / light- en Thou_ our / ev- 'ry heart, in-
shame / that carp- ing / doubts im- part, from

spire / us by Thy / Grace. The_ / face. O
out / our souls ef- /

Lord, the On- ly One_ Thou art to whom we look_

_ for_ com - fort.

Jacob Ebert, 1601

70

Du Grosser Schmerzensmann
Thou Mighty Man Of Woe

B. A. 39, N° 47

M. Janus, 1663

Thou Man of might-y woe, which God hast cast__ up-
on Thee! Ah Christ, we thank Thee so, for all the ev - il
done Thee, for all Thy soul's de-spair, when Thou wast cru - ci-
fied, for tor-ture, stripes and chains, and that for us Thou died.

Adam Thebesius † 1652

71

Du, o schönes Weltgebäude
Thou, O Beautiful Wordly Edifice

B. A. 39, N° 48

Johan Crüger, 1649

O thou world so fair - ly build - ed, oth - ers
All thy gold is on - ly gild - ed, stir - ring

may de - light in thee; Ye who reck - on Hea - ven hate -
naught but fear in me.

ful, keep the joys, to you so grate - ful. For Thy love a -

lone I pine, fair - est Je - sus, Je - sus mine.

Johann Franck, 1649

84

72

Du, o schönes Weltgebäude
Thou, O Beautiful Worldy Edifice

Cantata 56. Ich will den Kreuzstab gerne tragen

I Will Gladly Bear The Cross

B. A. 12, II, 104

Johann Crüger, 1649

Come, O Death, and end my__ voy - age,
Furl my sail and drop my__ an - chor,

make my jour - ney__ smooth and short.
bring me safe - ly__ in - to port.

Oth - ers__ shun and dread to meet Thee,
I with__ hear - ty joy will greet Thee.

Tis through death that I ac - quire Je - sus, Thee, my heart's de - sire.

Johann Franck, 1649

85

73

Durch Adams Fall is ganz verderbt
Through Adam's Fall All Is Corrupted

Cantata 18. Gleich wie der Regen und Schnee
Just As The Rain And Snow

Jos. Klug G.B. 1535

B. A. 2, 252

Old
With

A - dam's fall cor - rup - ted all, be -
sting drove hence our in - no - cence, nor
I be nev - er led a - stray, nor

fouled man's soul and stained it. The gained it. A -
have we yet and re - guide me, That vide me, My
by Thy Word Thou di -

1. & 3.
2. & 4.

- lone God's Grace may now e - rase our ru - in and dis -
sins ef - face and in Thy Grace, be Thou my trust - ed

hon - or. The snake de - ceived and temp - ted Eve, and
Mas - ter. Of mer - cy sure, make me se - cure from

brought God's wrath up - on her.
death and all dis - as - ter.

Lazarus Spengler, 1524

74

Ein' feste Burg ist unser Gott
A Mighty Fortress Is Our God

B. A. 39, N° 49

Jos. Klug G.B. 1535

A might-y fort-ress is our God, whose might will nev-er
keeps us free from all the horde of trou-bles that as-

1. fail us. He
2. sail us. Our old ev-il foe would fain

work us woe. With might and deep guile, he plans his pro-jects

vile; on earth is not one like him.

Martin Luther, 1529

87

75

Ein' feste Burg ist unser Gott
A Mighty Fortress Is Our God

B. A. 39, N° 50

Jos. Klug G. B. 1535

A might-y fort-ress is our God, whose might will nev-er fail us. Our
keeps us free from all the horde of trou-bles that as-sail us. Our old ev-il
foe would fain work us woe. With might and deep guile, he plans his
pro-jects vile. On earth is not one like him.

Martin Luther, 1529

76

Ein' feste Burg ist unser Gott
A Mighty Fortress Is Our God

Cantata 80. Ein' feste Burg is unser Gott

A Mighty Fortress Is Our God

B. A. 18, 378

Joh. Klug G. B. 1535

The Word of God_ will firm a - bide, a - gainst our foe's as -
He will bat - tle on our side, an Al - ly nev - er

sail - ing. For fail - ing. Tho' they take from me here all that

I hold dear, I will not com - plain; their van - tage

will_ be vain. God's might is all - pre - vail - ing.

Martin Luther, 1529

89

77

Eins is noth, ach Herr, dies Eine
One Thing Is Needed, O Lord, This One

Joach. Neander, 1680 (1679)

Freylingshausens G. B. 1704

B. A. 39, N° 51

One thing, Lord, to me is need-ful, teach me this one thing to know;

all things else seem vain and fu-tile, but a bur-den, fraught with woe.

These things on - ly scar the heart, plague it, and

pain it, and noth - ing of joy in the end do they

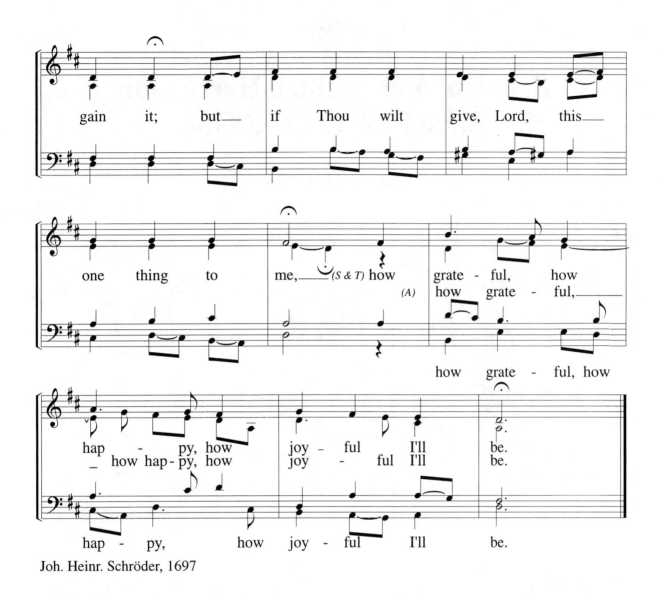

gain it; but___ if Thou wilt give, Lord, this___
one thing to me,___ *(S & T)* how grate - ful, how
(A) how grate - ful,___
how grate - ful, how
hap - py, how joy - ful I'll be.
___ how hap - py, how joy - ful I'll be.
hap - py, how joy - ful I'll be.

Joh. Heinr. Schröder, 1697

78

Erbarm' dich mein, o Herre Gott
Have Pity, O Lord God

B. A. 39, N° 52

Joh. Walther, 1524

Have pi - ty, Lord, thy ser - vant pleads, and throughThy love and
pure and clean all my mis - deeds, which well I know are

sav - ing Grace wash gross and base. My sin - ful soul I

can - not cure, nor wipe my ev - il deeds a-way; but e - vil Thou wilt

not en - dure, and Thou art just, what-ev - er men may say.

Erhart Hegenwalt, 1524

79

Erhalt' uns, Herr, bei deinem Wort
Sustain Us, Lord, By Thy Word

Cantata 6. Bleib bei uns, denn es Abend werden

Remain With Us, Then It Will Be Evening

B. A. 1,   176

Jos. Klug G. B. 1535

Sustain us,— Lord, Omnipotent, and smite all them on evil bent; all who Thy Kingdom would— disown, and cast Thy Son from off His Throne.

Make— manifest Thy— might, that Thou the Lord of Lords may ever— be; uphold Thy— Church— that we— may praise Thy Name through all Eternity.

Martin Luther, 1541

80
Ermuntre dich, mein schwacher Geist
Bestir Thyself, My Feeble Soul

Weinachts-Oratorium
Christmas Oratorio

B. A. 5 II, 59

Joh. Schop, 1641

Be- stir thy- self,_ my fee- ble soul, and come with ju- bi-
greet the lit- tle Je- sus Child with joy and a- do-
Break forth, O beau- teous morn- ing light, and fill theheav'ns with
shep-herd folk,_ re- strain your fright, and hear the An- gels'

1. & 3.
2. & 4.

la - tion to ra - tion. This is the night on which_ He came, and
glo- ry! Ye sto- ry: That this weak lit- tle ba- by boy shall

took a hu- man form and frame; the Fa- ther's Son with-
be our com- fort and our joy. A- gainst the Fiend sus-

in it, to woo the world and_ win it..
tain us, and peace at last will_ gain us.

Joh. Rist, 1641

94

81

Ermuntre dich, mein schwacher Geist
Bestir Thyself, My Feeble Soul

Cantata 43. Gott fähret auf mit Jauchzen
God Ascends With Cries Of Joy

Joh. Schop, 1641   B. A. 10,   126

Lord Je - sus Christ,___ Thou Prince of Love, when
Thou didst re - turn___ to God a - bove and
Draw us to Thee,___ and draw Thou near; give
That we may soar far, far from here to

past Thy re - sur - rec - tion.
those of His e - lec - tion.
us an ea - gle's pin - ions.
Hea - ven's high do - min - ions.

For Thy stu - pen - dous vic - to - ry,
O Lord, when may I come___ to Thee,

o - ver a might - y e - ne - my, which Thou hast
where I may e - ver joy - ful be? When shall I

gained in splen - dor, our heart - y praise we ren - der.
stand be - fore Thee, to wor - ship and a - dore Thee?

Joh. Rist, 1641

82
Ermuntre dich, mein schwacher Geist
Bestir Thyself, My Feeble Soul

Cantata 11. Lobet Gott in seinem Reichen
Praise God In His Kingdom

Joh. Schop, 1641

B.A. 2, 32

Ru - ler art Thou___ of earth and sky, the
Hi - ther and yon___ the An - gels fly, at

Fa - ther of Cre - a - tion.
Thy di - vine dic - ta - tion.

Prin - ces, o - be - dient to___ Thy Word,

own Thee their sov' - reign o - ver - lord. Earth, air and

fire and wa - ter, all bow to Thy might - y___ will.

Joh. Rist, 1641

96

83

Erschienen ist der herrlich' Tag
Now Dawns For Us The Glorious Day

Cantata 67. Halt im Gedächtniss Jesum Christ
Keep Jesus Christ In Your Mind

B. A. 16, 233

Nic. Hermann, 1560

Now dawns for us a glo - rious day, whose

joy no pow - er can gain - say. Our Bless - ed

Lord tri - um - phant rose, vic - to - rious o - ver

all His foes. A - le - lu - ja!

Nic. Hermann, 1560

84

Erschienen ist der herrlich' Tag
Now Dawns For Us A Glorious Day

Cantata 145. So du mit deinem Munde

So Thou With Thy Mouth

B. A. N° 30, 122

Nic. Herman, 1560

Joy-ful we hail this glo-rious day, sing-ing our Hal - le-lu-jas gay; with voi - ces all_ in sweet ac - cord, we join to praise our ri - sen Lord. Hal - le-lu - ja!

Nic.Herman, 1560

85

Erstanden ist der heilig' Christ
The Blessed Christ Is Risen

Triller, 1535

B. A. 39, N° 53

The Bless - ed Christ is ris'n to - day, al - le - lu - ja, al - le - lu - ja! Of all man - kind to be the Stay, al - le - lu - ja, al - le - lu - ja!

Arrangement of the hymn: Surexit Christus hodia

86

Es ist das Heil uns kommen her
Salvation Is Coming To Us

Cantata 86. Wahrlich ich sage euch
Verily, I Say Unto You

Wittenberg, 1524

B. A. 20 I, 134

Sal - va - tion sure has come to Man, the Grace of God pre - vail - eth. With Faith to Je - sus Christ we owe, from Him our ma - ny bless - ings flow, His Mer - cy nev - er fail - eth.

In out True Faith no hu - man plan nor mor - tal work a - vail - eth. Our know - ing what for us is best, the guile of foes will He ar - rest, if on - ly we will trust Him.

hope we wait the joy - ful day, for our as - sured sal - va - tion; But

when 'twill be God does not say, nor give an in - di - ca - tion. Well

1. & 3.
2. & 4.

Paul Speratus, 1523

100

87

Es ist das Heil uns kommen her
Salvation Is Coming To Us

Cantata 9. Es ist das Heil

It Is Salvation

B. A. 1, 274

Wittenberg, 1524

Though pray - ers be de - nied to you, be not ye then af - fright - ed, For
God re - mains for - ev - er true, in love with us u - nit - ed. Hold

ye then stead - fast to His Word, let not your hearts with doubt be stirred, nor think that you are slight - ed.

Paul Speratus, 1523

101

88

Es ist das Heil us kommen her
Salvation Is Coming To Us

Cantata 155. Mein Gott, wie lang', ach lange
My God, How Long

B. A. 32, 96

Wittenberg, 1524

Though pray - ers be de - nied to you, be
God re - mains for - ev - er true, in

1. not ye then af - fright - ed, For
   love with us u -
2. nit - ed. Hold

ye then stead - fast to His Word, let not your hearts with

doubt be stirred, nor think that you are slight - ed.

Paul Speratus, 1524

89

Es ist das Heil uns kommen her
Salvation Is Coming To Us

Trauungschoral
Wedding Chorale

B. A. 13 I, 148

Wittenberg, 1524

All glo - ry to the Lord of Lords, the
joy and hope to Man af - fords, in

Fa - ther of Cre - a - tion, Who sta - tion. Our
ev - 'ry rank and

1.

2.

cup to o - ver - flow - ing fills, and all our woe and

wail - ing stills; to Him be all the glo - ry.

Joh. Jac. Schütz, 1673

90

Es ist das Heil uns kommen her
Salvation Is Coming To Us

Cantata 117. Sei Lob und Ehr'dem höchsten Gut
Let Praise And Honor To The Highest Good

B. A. 24, 172

Wittenberg, 1524

I call to Thee in my dis - tress, O
me not know_ death's hope - less - ness, de -
Be - fore God's Pre - sence here we come in
du - ty own_ to Christ - en - dom, and

hear_ my_ sup - pli - ca - tion. Let
ny_ me not sal - la - tion. Our
loud - ly_ voiced e - la - tion. Our
sing_ in a - do -

va - tion. For
ra - tion. His

this my thanks go out_ to Thee. Come thank ye all our_
lov - ing care and o - ver - sight, is al - ways just and_

God with me! To Him_ be all the glo - ry.
al - ways right. To Him_ be all the glo - ry.

Joh. Jac. Schütz, 1662

91
Es ist genug
It Is Enough

Cantata 60. O Ewigkeit, du Donnerwort
O Eternity, Thou Thunder -Word

Joh. Rud. Ahle, 1662

B. A. 12 II, 190

Lyrics:
It is e-nough; so take my soul to Thee, with
It is e-nough; Lord, when it pleas-es Thee, do

Thine_ e - lect to be. Loose Thou my bonds, and set my
Thou_ un - shack-le me. My Je - sus comes; I bid the

spi - rit free; O God,_ de - liv - er me. I yearn for
world fare-well, and go_ in peace to dwell. In Hea - ven's

Thee, a - wake or sleep - ing; by day in tears, by night in
house I soon will find me, my cares and trou - bles all be -

weep - ing. It is e - nough, it is e - nough.
hind me. It is e - nough, it is e - nough.

Franz Joach. Burmeister, 1662

92

Es spricht der Unweisen Mund wohl
The Foolish Mouth Speaks Well

Joh. Walther, G. B. 1524

B. A. 39, N° 55

Their tongues in spe - cious words are skilled, with
hearts with un - be - lief are filled, their

grace to for - ti - fy them. Their
e - vil deeds be -

1. lie them. Their

2.

minds are rot - ten to the core, and all their ways does

God ab - hor; to good they ne'er ap - ply them.
ne'er ap-ply them.

Martin Luther, 1524

93

Es steh'n vor Gottes Throne
Standing Before God's Throne

B. A. 39, N° 56

Joach. à Burck, 1594

Before the Throne in Hea - ven, the Throne of God in
thro' His Son, the Fa - ther, our God and Lord, the

Hea - ven, our Guar - dians we will find, Where kind. Not
Fa - ther, loves tru - ly all man

one in all Cre - a - tion holds here so low a sta - tion, that

he will be de - spised, ne - glec - ted or de - spised.

Ludwig Helmbold, 1585

94

Es wird schier der letzte Tag herkommen
The Last Day Will Soon Be Here

B. A. 39, N° 57

Michael Weisse, 1531

Soon our fi - nal__ ho - ur will be__ sound - ing,

sins with us are more and more a - bound - ing.

What our Lord__ fore - told__ of yore, now we all de - plore.

Michael Weisse, 1531

95
Es woll' uns Gott genädig sein
May God Be Gracious To Us

B. A. 39, N° 58

Strassbourg Ministry, 1524

May God to us His Grace con - vey, His
shin - ing Face to light our way, to

Bless-ing on us cast - ing; His
glo - ry ev - er last - ing, That

we may un - der - stand His works and who on earth a - dore Him; That

Je - sus Christ at last may lead the Hea - then who ig -

nore Him to bow them down be - fore Him. Him.

Martin Luther, 1524

96
Es woll' uns Gott genädig sein
May God Be Gracious To Us

Strassbourg Ministry, 1524

B. A. 39, N° 59

Lyrics:

May God to us His Grace convey, His
shining face to light our way, His

blessings on us casting; His
glory ev-er-

lasting, That we may under-
stand His works and

who on Earth a-dore Him; That
Je-sus Christ at last may lead the Hea-then who ig-

nore Him to bow them down be-fore Him.
Him.

Martin Luther, 1524

110

97

Es woll' uns Gott genädig sein
May God Be Gracious To Us

Cantata 69. Lobe den Herren, meine Seele

Praise The Lord, My Soul

B. A. 16, 325

Strassbourg Ministry, 1524

Thy Name, O Lord, we magnify, and thank Thee, Thine elected. Our

flocks are fair, our crops are high, and Thy Word is well respected. We

bless Thee, Father, and Thy Son, the Holy Ghost, the Three-in-One; To

Them by all is honor done, Thy folk revere Thee ev'ry one, and from our hearts sing Amen.

Martin Luther, 1524

111

98

Freu dich sehr, o meine Seele
Rejoice Greatly, O My Soul

Cantata 70. Wachet, betet, seid bereit
Awake, Pray, Be Prepared

B. A. 16, 354

French Psalms, Geneva, 1551

1&2 Glad re - joice, my spi - rit to - day; cast a - side all
Christ the Lord now calls you a - way; bids you leave this

care and fears.
Vale of Tears.

1) Out from woe and sore dis - tress,
2) There with Him in joy to see,

forth to joy and bless - ed - ness, joy un - heard of, joy tran -
His ex - al - ted Ma - jes - ty, mid the An - gel Co - gre -

scend - ing, ev - er - last - ing, ne - ver end - ing.
ga - tion, in e - ter - nal a - do - ra - tion.

1620

99

Freu dich sehr, o meine Seele
Rejoice Greatly, O My Soul

Cantata 19. Es erhub sich ein Streit
A Dispute Arose

French Psalms, Geneva, 1551   B. A. 16, 354

Let   Thine An - gels   not   for - sake   me,   but   to
May   E - li - as'   char - iot   take   me,   There, like

Thee,   when life shall   cease. Let   me   rest   in   Thine em - brace.
La - za - rus in   peace.

Fill   my   heart with joy and   grace. When   my   days   on   earth are

end - ed,   may   my   soul with Thee   be blend - ed.

1620

100

Freu' dich sehr, o meine Seele
Rejoice Greatly, O My Soul

Cantata 194. Höchst erwünschtes Freudenfest
Greatly Desired Festival Of Joy

B. A. 29, 124

French Psalms, Geneva, 1551

God, to Thee must | I, com-plain-ing, | tell Thee all my | mi - se - ry.
My de-spair needs | no ex-plain-ing, | bet-ter known to | Thee than me.
Ho - ly Ghost, en - | throned in Hea-ven, | with the Fa-ther | and the son.
Hope and joy of | all af - flic-ted, | ev - er Bless-ed | Three - in - One.
Send Thy help, so | oft en-treat-ed, | no-ble Guest,Thou, | of my heart.
See Thy work, be - | gun, com-plet-ed, | nor from this, Thy | home, de - part.

Weak am I, this | well I know, | tempt-ed, wa-ver | to and fro.
Faith and hope and | cha - ri - ty, | Thou hast kin-dled | bright in me.
Fan the flame of | faith to fire, | that to hea - ven | I as-pire.

From my heart would | Sa-tan drive | me. Of my | faith would he de-prive me.
Help Thou me in | high en-dea - | vor. Watch Thou | o - ver me for - ev - er.
Gain the goal so | long ex-pec - | ted, There with | Thee and thine e - lec-ted.

Joh. Heerman, 1630

101
Freu dich sehr, o meine Seele
Rejoice Greatly, O My Soul

Cantata 25. Es ist nicht Gesundes an meinem Leibe
My Body Is Not Healthy

French Psalms, 1551

B. A. 5 I, 188

Ev - 'ry day my thanks re - dou - bles for Thy Hand, my
That my grie - vous cares and trou - bles Thou hast whol - ly

strength and stay. Ev - er while a - live and whole,
turned a - way.

Thy re - nown I will ex - tol. Wel - come soon my

li - be - ra - tion, in e - ter - nal a - do - ra - tion.

Joh. Heermann, 1630

102

Freu' dich sehr, o meine Seele
Rejoice Greatly, O My heart

Cantata 32. Liebster Jesu, mein Verlangen

Dearest Jesus, My Desire

B. A. 7, 80

French Psalms, Geneva, 1551

Put a - way, my heart, sus - pi - cion; God has not re -
To His Faith di - rect thy vi - sion, heed not them who
O - pen, Lord, to me the por - tals of Thy Good - ness
Let me taste Thy ten - der sweet - ness, ev - 'ry hour, in

jec - ted Thee.
dis - a - gree.
and thy Grace
ev - 'ry place.

Hast thou trod the e - vil path?
Love me, Lord, and day by day,

Hast de - served to feel His wrath? Think - est thou His_
guide me that, as best I may, In my heart I_

heart is hard - ened? Nay,_ de - spair not, thou art par - doned.
shall re - ceive Thee, Nor_ do aught a - miss to grieve_ Thee.

Paul Gerhardt, 1648

116

103
Freu' dich sehr, o meine Seele
Rejoice Greatly, O My Soul

Cantata 30. Freue dich, erlöste Schaar

Rejoice, Redeemed Flock

B. A. 5 I, 360

French Psalms, Geneva, 1551

"Be con-soled, be not de-spair - ing, ye my
Hope-ful, ye who now are bear - ing scorn and
Hark, I hear the voice that cri - eth far a -
"Swift pre-pare the Lord a path - way, make ye

peo - ple," saith the Lord.
shame from Sa - tan's horde.   If Je-ru-sa-lem be near,
cross the de-sert waste: Le-vel make ye ev-'ry hill,
straight His way with haste.

speak to her a word of cheer; For her cou - rage,
ev - 'ry dale and val - ley fill; Make ye smooth the

her en-du - rance, of de - liv'-rance gives as - sur - ance.
rough-est spa - ces, straigh-ten ye the crook-ed pla - ces."

Joh. Olearius

117

104

Freu' dich sehr, o meine Seele
Rejoice Greatly, O My Soul

Cantata 39. Brich dem Hungrigen dein Brot
Break Thy Bread With The Hungry

B. A. 7, 348

French Psalms, Geneva, 1551

Come and suf-fer Christ to teach you, come and learn ye
Let His Ho-ly Gos-pel reach you, ye who Christ,your
Bless-ed they who from com-pas-sion help to stran-ger
With the need-y share their ra-tion, pray de-vout-ly

from Him now. Ye who would His Word re-ceive,
Lord a-vow.
folk af-ford. They who help by word and deed,
to the Lord.

in your heart of hearts be-lieve; Ye,— who, while you—
neigh-bors in their time of need, They— who prac-tice—

live, en-dea-vor Him— to serve with good deeds ev-er.
true com-pas-sion, God will serve in e-qual fash-ion.

Dav. Denicke, 1676

105

Freuet euch, ihr Christen alle
Rejoice, All You Christians

Cantata 40. Dazu ist erschienen

Here Has Appeared

B. A. 7, 394

Andr. Hammerschmidt, 1646

Joy - ful sing ye, Chris - tian peo - ple, loud re joice with one ac - cord.
Je - sus, let Thou Thine e - lec - ted fur - ther in Thy fa - vor fare.

Hail ye Je - sus Christ the Lord. Sound the chimes from ev - 'ry stee - ple,
Hear Thou them and grant their pray'r. Quick - en all who are de - jec - ted,

deck the hearth with hol - ly gay, For to - day is Christ - mas Day.
give Thy folk all gath - ered here peace and joy this com - ing year.

Thro' the world glad tid - ings ring - ing, joy - ful mul - ti - tudes are sing - ing:
Joy - ful, joy - ful dawns the mor - row, Christ has ban - ished ev - 'ry sor - row.

Glo - ry, glo - ry to the High - est, peace on earth, good will to all men.
Rap - ture, rap - ture ev - er near - ing, see the Sun of Grace ap - pear - ing.

Christian Keymann, 1646

119

106

Für Freuden lasst uns springen
Let Us Jump For Joy

B. A. 39, N° 60

Casp. Peltsch, 1648

107

Gelobet seist du, Jesu Christ
Praised Be Thee, Jesus Christ

Joh. Walther G. B. 1524

B A. 39, N° 61

We praise Thee all, our Sa - viour dear, that as man Thou cam - est here. A Vir - gin bore Thee, that is clear; the joy - ful news the An - gels hear. Al - le - lu - ja!

Martin Luther, 1524

108

Gelobet seist du, Jesu Christ
Praised Be Thou, Jesus Christ

Cantata 64. Sehet, welch' eine Liebe
See, What A Love

Joh. Walther, G. B. 1524   B. A. 16, 118

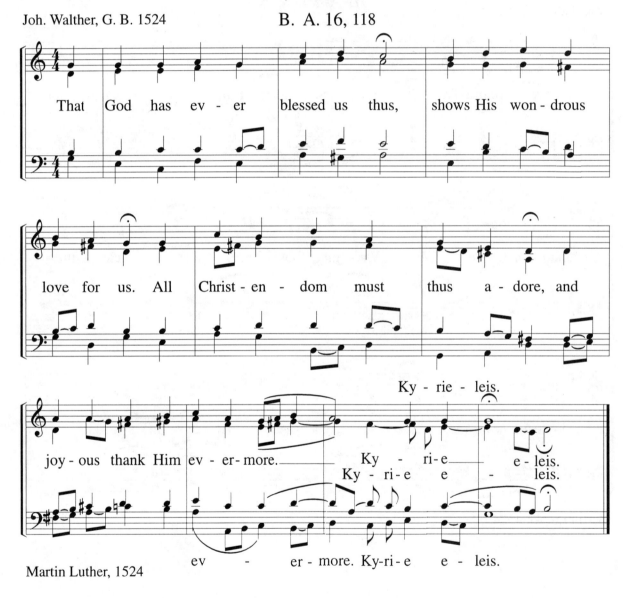

That God has ev - er blessed us thus, shows His won - drous
love for us. All Christ - en - dom must thus a - dore, and
joy - ous thank Him ev - er - more. Ky - ri - e e - leis.
Ky - rie - leis.
Ky - ri - e e - leis.
ev - er - more. Ky-ri - e e - leis.

Martin Luther, 1524

109

Gelobet seist du, Jesu Christ
Praised Be Thou, Jesus Christ

Cantata 91. Gelobet seist du, Jesus Christ
Praised Be Thou, Jesus Christ

Joh. Walther G. B. 1524

B. A. 22, 32

That God has ev- er blessed us thus, shows— His won- drous—

love for us. All Christ-en- dom must thus— a- dore, and

joy- ous thank Him e — ver- more. Ky- ri-e - leis!

e - ver- more.— Ky - ri-e - leis!

e - ver- more. Ky- ri-e - leis!

e — ver - more. Ky — ri — e- leis!

Martin Luther, 1524

110

Gelobet seist du, Jesus Christ
Praised Be Thou, Jesus Christ

Weihnachts-Oratorium

Christmas Oratorio

Joh. Walther G. B. 1524   B. A. 5 II, 110

Martin Luther, 1524

111

Gieb dich zufrieden und sei stille
Be Happy And Be Still

J. S. Bach, 1725

B. A. 39, N° 62

P. Gerhardt, 1666

112

Gott, der du selber bist das Licht
God, Who Art Thyself The Light

B. A. 39, N° 63

J. Crüger, 1648

O God, who art Thy - self the Light, through
Grace un - dy - ing we would praise, in

thine un - con - quer - ab - le might the
songs of thanks our voi - ces raise, that

dark of night is
Thou hast us be -

1. end - ed. Thy

2. friend - ed; That Thou a faith - ful

watch has kept, and guard - ed us, the while we slept.

Joh. Rist, 1641

113

Gott der Vater wohn' uns bei
God The Father Dwell In Us

Joh. Walther, 1524

B. A. 39, N° 64

Father, dwell in ev - 'ry heart, and save us from dam - na - tion.
Free from sin would we de - part, as - sured of Thy sal - va - tion.

Firm of faith, let us with - stand the De - vil's fell con-
Here to live as Thou com - mand. Pro - tect us and be-

triv - ing, our strength from Thee de - riv - ing, with
friend— us, lest Sa - tan's cun - ning rend— us. Thy

firm de - vo - tion striv - ing. A - men, thus it
might - y wea - pons send— us.

will be - fall, so Al - le - lu - ja sing we all.

Martin Luther, 1524

114

Gott des Himmels und der Erden
God Of Heaven and Earth

Weinachts-Oratorium

Christmas Oratorio

B. A. 5 II, 208

Heinr. Albert, 1644

115

Gottes Sohn ist kommen
God's Son Is Come

B. A. 39, N° 65

Michael Weisse, 1531

God's own Son ap - pear - eth, Man's sal - va - tion near - eth. O - pens Hea - ven's por - tal, Gains us Life Im - mor - tal. Hum - ble was His sta - tion, Us He brought sal - va - tion.

J. Horn, 1544

116

Gott hat das Evangelium
God Has Given The Gospel

B. A. 39, N° 66

Erasmus Alberus, 1548

The Gos - pel God has gi - ven you, to

make you pi - ous, good and true; But man does not re -

spect this boon, his re - tri - bu - tion will be soon. The

Judge - ment Day is now not far a - way.

Erasmus Alberus, 1548

117

Gott lebet noch
God Liveth Yet

Freilinghausen's G. B. II, 1548

B. A. 39, N° 67

Joh. Friedr. Zihn, 1692 (1682)

118

Gottlob, es geht nunmehr zu Ende
Thank God, The End Is At Hand

B. A. 39, N° 68

Probably by J. S. Bach

Thanks be to God, my end is near me,
Je - sus will com - fort me and cheer me,

soon will the strife for me be done.
Je - sus, who my sal - va - tion won.

Let me then die and go a - way;

"Je - sus," the word I last will say.
I last will say.

Christian Weise, 1682

119
Gott sei gelobet und gebenedeiet
God Be Praised And Blessed

J. Walther G. B. 1525

B. A. 39, N° 69

Come ye and praise Him, praise your God and bless
blood and bo - dy, so do you pos - sess

1.
Him, He who His own bo - dy gave you. His

2.
Him; gave Him - self for you to save you. Ky -

rie e - lei - son. By thy bo - dy which was pained

now

Mo-ther Ma-
sore, bo - dy which Thy Mo - ther Ma-ry bore; by Thy blood we now plead:

we now

Help us Lord, thro' all our need. Ky - rie e - lei - son.

Christian Weisse, 1682

120

Gott sei uns gnädig und barmherzig
God Be Gracious And Merciful To Us

G. Rhau, Enchiridion, 1535
Jos. Klug G. B. 1535

B. A. 39, N° 70

God.___ show us grace and lov - ing kind -

and give us Thy div - vine be - ne -
ness, and___ give us Thy di - vine be -
and_ give us Thy di - vine be -

dic - tion.
ne - dic - tion.
ne - dic - tion.

From 4, Moses, 6, 24-26

121

Meine Seele erhebt den Herren
My Soul Exhalts The Lord

G. Rhau, Enchiridion, 1535
and Jos. Klug G. B. 1535

B. A. 39, N° 71

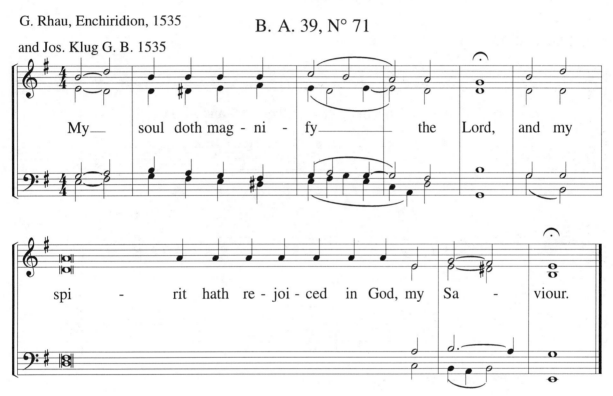

My soul doth mag - ni - fy the Lord, and my spi - rit hath re - joi - ced in God, my Sa - viour.

Luke 1, 46 and 47

122

Meine Seele erhebt den Herren
My Soul Exhalts The Lord

Cantata 10. Meine Seele erhebt den Herren

My Soul Exhalts The Lord

B. A. 1, 303

Jos. Klug G. B. 1535

Jos. Klug G. B. 1535

123a

Heilig, heilig
Holy, Holy

B. A. 39, N° 72

Handwritten Chorale Book, Steinau, 1726
Probably transformed by Bach

Holy, ho - ly, ho - ly, Lord God Thou of Sa - ba -

oth! All the Hea - vens ex - alt Thy Ma - jes - ty.

Sing Ho - san - na in the High - est. Ho - san - na, bless - ed he who

comes in Thy Name. Sing Ho - san - na in the High - est.

Jesse 6, 3 and Matthew 21, 9

123b

Sanctus, sanctus Dominus Deus Sabaoth
Holy, Holy, Lord God Of Sabaoth

B. A. 39, N° 72

Sanc-tus sanc - tus, sanc - tus Do - mi-nus De - us Sa - ba-

oth. Ple - ni sunt coe - li glo - ri - a tu - a.

O - san - na
O - san - na in ex - cel - sis. Be - ne - dic-tus, qui ve - nit in
O - san - na

no - mi-ne Do - mi - ni. O - san - na in ex - cel - sis!

124

Helft mir Gott's Güte preisen
Help Me to Praise God's Goodness

Cantata 28. Gottlob, nun geht das Jahr zu Ende
Praise God, Now The Year Is Ending

Wolfg. Figulus, 1575

B. A. 5 I, 272

Come sing ye, lit - tle chil - dren, come thank your God with
sing to praise His good - ness with love - ly me - lo -
Our God in Hea - ven reign - ing, we praise Thee, ev - 'ry -
all we are ob - tain - ing, through Je - sus Christ, Thy

me. Come
one. For
dy. Son. 'Twill
And soon be New Year's Day! The
so this pray - er hear: That

sun, for sum - mer yearn - ing, its leng - thened course is
peace and joy Thou send us, from ev - 'ry ill de -

turn - ing, with spring not far a - way.
fend us through out the com - ing year.

Paul Eber, before 1569

139

125

Helft mir Gott's Güte preisen
Help Me To Praise God's Goodness

Cantata 16. Herr Gott, dich loben wir
Lord God, We Praise Thee

B. A. 2, 198

Wolfg. Figulus, 1575

Come sing ye, lit - tle chil - dren, come thank your God with
sing to praise His good - ness with love - ly me - lo -

me. Come
dy. 'Twill soon be New Year's Day! The

sun for sum - mer yearn - ing, its length - ened course is

turn - ing, with spring not far a - way.

Paul Eber, before 1569

126

Helft mir Gott's Güte preisen
Help Me To Praise God's Goodness

Cantata 183. Sie werden euch in den Bann thun
You Shall Be Excommunicated

B. A. 37, 74

Wolfg. Figulus, 1575

Take Thine a - bode with - in me, my heart's be - lov - ed guest. As
mor - tal Thou didst win me new life and hope and zest. O
'Tis Thou, O Ho - ly Spi - rit, that teach - est us to pray. And
Thou, O Lord, will hear it, and speed our song a way to

1. & 3.
2. & 4.

guest. As zest. O well - be - lov - ed Three; The Fa ther, Son and
pray. And way to Thee in Hea ven High, Far up to Thee as -

Spi - rit, en - throned a - like in Hea - ven, in e - qual ma - jes - ty.
scend - ing, a cho - rus ne - ver end - ing, and heard be - yond the sky.

P. Gerhardt, 1653

127

Herr Christ, der einig' Gott's Sohn
Lord Christ, God's Only Son

Cantata 164. Ihr, die ihr euch von Christo nenne
You, Who Call Yourselves Christians

Erfurt Enchiridion, 1524

B. A. 33, 88

Lord Christ, by God en - gen - dered, our
Trans - form us by Thy kind - ness, a -
res - cue Man sur - ren - dered, as
we put on the New Man, the

1. & 3.

2. & 4.

Fa - ther ev - er - more, To yore. The
Scrip - ture told of grace, That face. While
wake us through Thy
Old Man's pow'r ef -

Star is He of morn - ing, His bright - ness Heav'n a -
here as mor - tals liv - ing, with hear - ti - est thanks -

dorn - ing, far bright - est star of all.
giv - ing, our trust in Thee we place.

Elisabeth Creutziger, 1524

142

128

Herr Christ, der einig' Gott's Sohn
Lord Christ, God's Only Son

Cantata 96. Herr Christ, der einig' Gott's Sohn
Lord Christ, God's Only Son

Erfurt Enchiridion, 1524   B A. 22, 184

Trans - form us by Thy kind - ness, a - wake us by Thy
we put on the New Man, the Old Man's pow'r ef -

grace, That face. While here as mor - tals liv - ing, with

hear - ti - est thanks - giv - ing, our trust in Thee we place.

Elisabeth Creutzinger, 1524

143

129

Herr Gott, dich loben alle wir
Lord God, We Praise Thee All

French Psalms, Geneva, 1551

B. A. 39, N° 73

Lord God, we praise Thee, all of
all___ of

us, with deep and heart - felt thank - ful -

ness, that Thou hast There an An - gel

Band to serve and guard at Thy com - mand.
Thy___ com - mand.

Paul Eber, 1554 (?)

130

Herr Gott, dich loben alle wir
Lord God, We Praise Thee All

French Psalms, Geneva, 1551

Lord God, we thank Thee, all of us, with

deep and heart-felt thank-ful-ness, That thou hast

There an An-gel Band to serve and guard at Thy com-mand

Paul Eber, 1554 (?)

131

Herr Gott, dich loben alle wir
Lord God, We Praise Thee All

Cantata 130. Herr Gott, dich lobe alle wir
Lord God, We Praise Thee All

French Psalms, Geneva, 1551

B. A. 26, 268

With   grate - ful   hearts   we   come   to
We   pray   Thee,   Lord,   do   Thou   to   com -

Thee,   to   ren - der   thanks   e - ter - nal -
mand   this   host   to   guard   us   faith - ful

ly,   And   with   the   An - gel   Host   a -
ly,   To   fight   our   foes,   their   guile   con -

dore,   and   praise____ Thee   now____ and   ev - er - more.
fute,   and   keep____ Thy   Word____ in   good   re - pute.

Paul Eber, 1554 (?)

132

Herr Gott, dich loben alle wir
Dear God, We Praise Thee All

B. A. 39, N° 74

French Psalms, Geneva, 1551

Before Thy Throne I come today, O God, and humble here I pray. Unworthy sinner though I be, turn not Thy gracious face from me.

Bodo von Hodenberg, 1648

133
Herr Gott, dich loben wir
Lord God, We Praise Thee

J. Klug G. B. 1535   B. A. 39, N° 75

Heav'n and earth de - clare to Thee. Lord Je - sus Christ, Thou
pro - phets and the mar - tyrs too, The Vir - gin's womb did
sing in praise of God the Lord. The might of death is
tid - ings of Thy glo - ry come. At God's right hand Thou
Ho - ly Ghost, the Three - in - One, Thou art the Judge whom
ser - vice true will join in praise. Now help, O Lord, Thy

Migh - ty One, the Fa - ther God's E - ter - nal Son,
not dis - dain sal - va - tion for man - kind to gain.
ren - dered naught, and Chris - tians all to Hea - ven brought.
sit test there, the hon - ors of His realm to share.
sin - ners dread, to judge the liv - ing and the dead.
ser - vants well, they whom Thy Blood has saved from Hell.

Let us of Hea-ven have a share with all the saints as - sem-bled there. Keep

us Thy Folk from Sa-tan's snares, and bless us, for we are Thine heirs. Pre-

pare us here to dwell with Thee, for Hea-ven and E-ter-ni-ty. Each

day, Lord God we wor-ship Thee, Thy Name we hon-or con-stant-ly.

Pre-serve us, Lord, to-day from greed, from sin and ev-'ry e-vil deed.
Be mer-ci-ful, O Lord, we plead, be mer-ci-ful to us in need.
Com-pas-sion-ate we pray Thee be, for all our hope de-pends on Thee.

And so we pray in Je-sus' Name, that we be ne-ver

A-men.

brought to shame. A-men.

Ambrosian hymn translated into German by Luther, 1529

150

134

Herr Gott, dich loben wir
Lord God, We Praise Thee

Cantata 119. Preise, Jerusalem, den Herrn

Glorify, Jerusalem, The Lord

J. Klug G. B. 1535

B. A. 24, 246

Preserve us, Jesus Christ, our Lord, Thy blessing to Thy Folk afford. Watch over us who Thee adore, and praise Thy Name forevermore. Amen.

Martin Luther, 1529

135

Herr Gott, dich loben wir
Lord God, We Praise Thee

Cantata 120. Gott, man lobet dich in der Stille
God, We Praise Thee In The Stillness

Val. Babst, 1545

B. A. 24, 284

Protect us, Lord, and be our Guide; it was for us the Saviour died. The

joys of Heaven let us share, to dwell with all Thy servants there. Pre-

serve us, Jesus Christ, our Lord, Thy Blessing to Thy Folk afford. Watch

over us who Thee adore, and praise Thy Name forevermore.

Martin Luther, 1529

136

Herr, ich denk' an jene Zeit
Lord, I Think Of That Time

B. A. 39, N° 76

G. B. of the Böhm brothers, 1566

Ev - er think I of That Day. Life is short and death is near - is near - ing. "Fare - thee - well, I go a - way," soon the world is hear - ing. I through death_ may con - quer still; by Thy will, ev - er per - se - ver - ing.

Georg. Mylius, 1630

137

Herr, ich habe missgehandelt
Lord, I Have Done Wrong

B. A. 39, N° 77

J. Krüger, 1649

Lord, my__ ev - il deeds__ are ma - ny, sore my vi - ces
I have__ wan - dered from__ the path - way that has been re -

would I hide me

bur - den me. Now in ter - ror would I hide_____ me
vealed by Thee.

would I hide me

from the wrath that will be - tide me.

J. Frank, before 1649

138

Herr, ich habe missgehandelt
Lord, I Have Done Wrong

B. A. 39, N° 78

J. Krüger, 1649

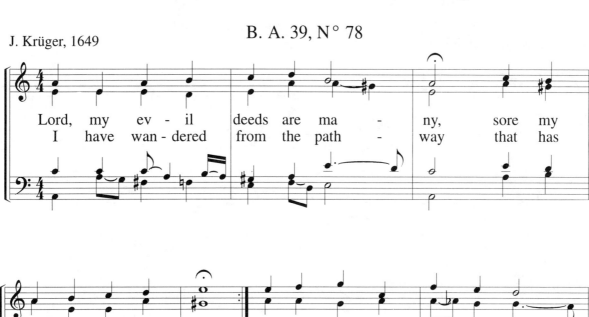

Lord, my ev - il deeds are ma - ny, sore my
I have wan - dered from the path - way that has

vi - ces bur - den me. Now in ter - ror would I hide
been re - vealed by Thee.

me from the wrath that will be - tide me

J. Frank, before 1649

139

Herr Jesu Christ, dich zu uns wend'
Lord Jesus Christ, Turn To Us

B. A. 39, N° 79

Pensum sacrum. Görlitz, 1648

Lord Je - sus Christ I turn to Thee, Thy

Ho - ly Spi - rit send to me. With help and grace lead

Thou the way, lest from the path of truth I stray.

Duke Wilhelm II zu Sachsen Weimar (?) 1651

140

Herr Jesu Christ, du hast bereit't
Lord Jesus Christ, Thou Hast Prepar'd

Manuscript: J. G. Wagner, 1742
(Perhaps by Bach)

B. A. 39, N° 80

Lord Je - sus Thou pre - pared a meal for
blood and bo - dy, true and real, and

us poor souls be - night - ed. Thy
us as guests in vit - ed. So

we who thus Thy guests have been, now pray Thee, "Lift this

load of sin, which all our lives has blight - ed."

Samuel Kinner, 1622

141

Herr Jesu Christ, du höchstes Gut
Lord Jesus Christ, Thou Highest Good

Dresden G. B. 1593

B. A. 39, N° 81

Lord Je - sus Christ, Thou Fount of Grace and Source of ev - 'ry
hold, I kneel be - fore Thy face, my load of sin con -

Bless - ing, Be - fess - ing. The darts of wrath from

out the blue have pierced my con - science_ through and through, to
my con - science thro' and thro'

pun - ish my_ trans - gress - ing.

Bartolomæus Ringwalt, 1588

142
Herr Jesu Christ, du höchstes Gut
Lord Jesus Christ, Thou Highest Good

Cantata 113. Herr Jesu Christ, du höchstes Gut
Lord Jesus Christ, Thou Highest Good

B. A. 24, 80

Dresden G. B. 1593

By Thine a - ton - ment make me strong, Thy love and grace re -
Thou my soul of ev - 'ry wrong, Of ev - 'ry tress - pass

veal me. Wash heal me. And take me when it

pleas - es Thee, In Hea - ven ev - er - more to be, With

Thee and Thine E - lec - ted.

Barth. Ringwalt, 1588

143

Herr Jesu Christ, du höchstes Gut
Lord Jesus Christ, Thou Highest Good

Cantata 168. Thue Rechnung! Donnerwort
Repent! Thunder-word

Dresden G. B. 1539

B. A. 33, 166

By Thine a - tone-ment make me strong, Thy love and grace re -
Thou my soul of ev - 'ry wrong, of ev - 'ry tress - pass

veal me. Wash heal me, And take me when it

pleas - es Thee, in Hea - ven ev - er - more to be, with

Thine E - lec - ted.
Thee and Thine E - lec - ted.

Bartholomæus Ringwalt, 1588

144
Herr Jesu Christ, du höchstes Gut
Lord Jesus Christ, Thou Highest Good

Cantata 48. Ich elender Mensch, wer wird mich erlösen

I, Miserable Man, Who Will Redeem Me?

Dresden G. B. 1593

B. A. 10, 298

Lord Je - sus Christ, I cry to Thee, in woe all woe ex -
Thou Thy Grace de - scend on me, and make my heart Thy
My heart, O Lord, is sore dis - tressed by all the woes that
since to Thee tis man - i - fest, Thou canst and wilt re -

1. & 3.

cell - ing. Let
grieve it, And

2. & 4.

dwell - ing. The great and griev - ous
lieve it. So at Thy side I

care and pain which rends my heart with might and main, is
take my stand, my heart I place at Thy com-mand; do

past all mor - tal tell - ing.
Thou in grace re - ceive it.

J. H. Schein's Cantional (?)

145

Herr Jesu Christ, mein's Lebens Licht
Lord Jesus Christ, Light Of My Life

Seth Calvisius, 1594
(Rex Christe factor omnium)

B. A. 39, N° 82

O   Je - sus Christ,   my   life,___ my   light,   my___
O   Je - sus, Thou,   my   heart's___ de - light,   who___

joy,   my peace, my   com - fort bright, On   earth I   here   am
by   Thy Cross and   bit - ter plight, Through   death hast   my   Re -

but   a   guest, by___   hea - vy   load   of   sin___ op - pressed.
deem - er   been, Thy___   love did   lift   a   load___ of   sin.

M. Behm, 1610

146

Herr Jesu Christ, wahr'r Mensch und Gott
Lord Jesus Christ, True Man And God

Polish cantional, 1559
Joh. Eccard, 1597

B. A. 39, N° 83

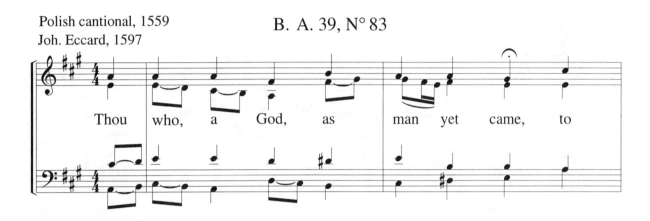

Thou who, a God, as man yet came, to

suf - fer mar - tyr - dom and shame, Up - on the Cross at

last wast slain, the Fa - ther's grace for me to gain.

P. Eber, 1560

147

Herr Jesu Christ, wahr'r Mensch und Gott
Lord Jesus Christ, True Man And God

Cantata 127. Herr Jesu Christ, wahr'r Mensch und Gott
Lord Jesus Christ, True Man And God

B. A. 26, 160

French Psalms, Geneva, 1555

Ah Lord, for - give us all our guilt, and grant us mor - tals

if Thou wilt, That pa - tient we may bear our lot, with

stead - fast faith that fal - ters not, In firm re - li - ance

on Thy love, un - til we come to Thee a - bove.

P. Eber, 1560

148

Herr, nun lass in Friede
Lord, Now Leave In Peace

B. A. 39, N° 84

Böhm brothers, 1694

Lord, in peace de - part I;   faint and sick at   heart I.

Forth to Hea - ven far - ing,   with Thine An - gels shar - ing

peace be - yond all   mea - sure,   if it be Thy   plea - sure.

David Behme, before 1657

165

149

Herr, straf' mich nicht in deinem Zorn
Lord, In Anger Smite Me Not

B. A. 39, N° 85

J. Crüger, 1640

Lord God, in an - ger smite me not; this
whol - ly hope - less is my lot, for

from my heart I pray Thee, Else
I may not gain-

say Thee. Re -

pen - tant, tru - ly have I been, and suf - fered sore - ly

from my sin; Let this, O Lord, al - lay Thee.

1640 (?)

150

Herr, wie du willst, so schick's mit mir
(Aus tiefer Noth schrei' ich zu dir)
Lord, As Thou Wilt, So May It Be
(From Deep Affliction I Cry To Thee)

Cantata 156. Ich steh' mit einem Fuss im Grabe
I Am Standing With One Foot In The Grave

Strassbourg Ministry, 1521

B. A. 32, 114

Lord, as Thou wilt, so may it be, in Life and Death
hope and joy is all in Thee, Lord, Thou wilt not

- pro - tect me. My
re - ject

me. Up - hold me by Thy

Sav - ing Grace, else make me brave, the trials to face, for

which Thou may se - lect me.

Caspar Bienemann, 1574

167

151

Herr, wie du willst, so schick's mit mir
(Aus tiefer Noth schrei' ich zu dir)

Lord, As Thou Wilt, So May It Be
(From Deep Affliction I Cry To Thee)

Strassbourg, 1525

B. A. 39, N° 86

Lord, as Thou willt, so may it be; in
My hope and joy is all in Thee, Lord,
Whom migh - ty God will watch and ward, in
May say: Thou art my ha - ven, Lord, in my

Life and Death pro - tect me. Up - hold_ me
Thou wilt not re - ject me. For Thou_ wilt
all with Him a - gree - ing.
God, my hope, my_ Be - ing.

by_ Thy sav - ing grace, else make me brave, the
sure - ly res - cue me from Sa - tan's shack - les

trials to face, for which Thou may se - lect_ me.
gra - cious - ly, from pes - ti - lence_ will_ free me.

Caspar Bienemann, 1574

152

Herzlich lieb hab' ich dich, o Herr
I Love Thee, Lord, With All My Heart

B. A. 39, N° 87

Pasch. Reinigius, 1587

B. Schmid, Tablature Book, 1577

I love Thee, Lord, with all my heart, and pray Thee, stay Thou
ask for no - thing here on earth, the whole world seems of

not a - part, but help me, Lord, and bless me. I
lit - tle worth, if I, Lord, but pos-
sess Thee When grief is like to

break my heart, then Thou my firm re - li - ance art. My hope and com - fort

Thou wilt be, Thou who wert cru - ci - fied for me. Lord Je - sus Christ, ask

Thou the Fa - ther in Thy Name, that ne - ver I be brought to shame.

Martin Schalling, 1571

153
Herzlich lieb hab' ich dich, o Herr
I Love Thee, Lord, With All My Heart

Cantata 174. Ich liebe den Höchsten
I Love The Highest One

Pasch. Reinigius, 1587 B. A. 35, 157 B. Schmid, Tablature Book,1577

I love Thee, Lord, with all my heart, and pray Thee, stay Thou
ask for no- thing here on earth, the whole world seems of

not a- part, but help me Lord, and bless me. I
lit- tle worth, if I, Lord, but pos-

1. sess Thee. When grief is like to
2.

break my heart, then Thou my firm re- li- ance art. My Hope and Com- fort

Thou wilt be, Thou who wast cru - ci - fied for me. Lord Je - sus Christ, ask

Thou the Fa - ther in Thy Name, that nev- er I be brought to shame.

Martin Schalling, 1571

170

154
Herzlich lieb hab ich dich, o Herr
I Love Thee, Lord With All My Heart

Johannes-Passion
St. John Passion
B. A. 12 I, 131

Pasch. Reinigius, 1587

B. Schmid, Tablature Book, 1577

O Lord, when comes that final day, may Angels bear my
then my body's anguish cease, that it may rest in

soul away, to Abram's bosom take it. Let
painless peace, til Thou again awake

it. Ah, what a joy it then will be, the Very Son of God to see, and

there to meet Him face to face, my Saviour on the Throne of Grace! Lord

Jesus Christ, now hear Thou me! O hear Thou me! Thy Name I praise eternally!

Martin Schalling, 1571

155
Herzlich lieb hab ich dich, o Herr
I Love Thee, Lord, With All My Heart

Cantata 149. Man singet mit Freuden vom Sieg
With Joy We Sing Of The Victory

Pasch. Reinigius, 1587   B. A. 30, 299   B. Schmid, Tablature Book, 1577

O Lord, when comes_ that Fi - nal Day, may An - gels bear_ my
then my bo - dy's an - guish cease, that it may rest_ in

soul a - way, to A - bram's bos - om take it. Let wake it. Ah,
pain - less peace, til Thou a - gain a -

what a joy_ it_ then will be, the Ve - ry Son_ of_ God to see, and

there_ to meet_Him face to face, my Sa - viour on the Throne of Grace! Lord

Je - sus Christ, O hearThou me,_O hearThou me! Thy Name I praise e - ter - nal-ly.

Martin Schalling, 1571

172

156
Herzlich thut mich verlangen
My Heart Is Ever Yearning

Cantata 135. Ach Herr, mich armen Sünder
O Lord, I Poor Sinner

Hans Leo Hassler, 1601

B. A. 28, 136

Though
All

tem - per Thou Thy
glo - ry to the
Ho - ly Ghost we

sin - ner, in
Fa - ther, all
hon - or, the

1. & 3.
an - ger smite me
hope - less is my
glo - ry to the

not, And
Son. The

2. & 4.
lot. O
One. The

Lord, I pray for - give me, for - give and wel - come
Fa - ther, Son and Spi - rit, for - ev - er we a -

me, to dwell for - ev - er with Thee, from
dore; on high in Hea - ven reign - ing, hence -

hence -

tor - ment free.

Hell and tor - ment free.
forth for ev - er - more.

forth

for ev - er - more.

Cyriacus Schneegass, 1597

173

157

Herzlich thut mich verlangen
My Heart Is Ever Yearning

Hans Leo Hassler, 1601

B. A. 39, N° 18

En - trust thy ways un - to Him, and all thy spi - rit
ev - er faith - ful Guar - dian, who rules the winds and

craves; The waves, Who guides the clouds of Hea - ven, and

bids the breez - es blow. He best can choose the

path - way on which our steps shall go.

our steps shall go.

P. Gerhardt, 1656

158

Herzlich thut mich verlangen
My Heart Is Ever Yearning

B. A. 39, N° 19

Hans Leo Hassler, 1601

En - trust thy ways un - to Him, and all thy spi - rit
ev - er faith - ful Guar - dian, who guides the winds and

craves, The waves, Who rules the clouds of Hea - ven, and

bids the breez - es blow; He best can choose the

shall go.

path - way on which our steps shall go.

P. Gerhardt, 1656

159

Herzlich thut mich verlangen
My Heart Is Ever yearning

Mattäus-Passion

St. Matthew Passion

Hans Leo Hassler, 1601

B. A. 4, 186

En - trust thy ways un - to Him, and all thy spi - rit
ev - er faith - ful Guar - dian, who guides the winds and

craves, The waves, Who rules the clouds of Hea - ven, and

bids the breez - es blow; He best can choose the

path way, on which our steps shall go.

P. Gerhardt, 1656

160

Herzlich thut mich verlangen
My Heart Is Ever Yearning

Cantata 153. Schau, lieber Gott, wie meine Feind
See, Dear God, How Mine Enemies

Hans Leo Hassler, 1601

B. A. 32, 46

Though all the fiends are striv - ing, o'er Hea - ven to pre -
vain their fell con - triv - ing, their Hell - ish plot will

vail, All fail. What God has well pro - vid - ed, no

mor - tal can a - mend, And what He has de -

cid - ed, will hap - pen in the end.

P. Gerhardt, 1656

161

Herzlich thut mich verlangen
My Heart Is Ever Yearning

Cantata 161. Komm, du süsse Todesstunde

Come, Thou Sweet Hour Of Death

B. A. 33, 27

Hans Leo Hassler, 1601

My heart is ev - er yearn - ing for bless - ed death's re -
ills that here sur - round me, and woes that nev - er
Though worms our flesh de - vo - ur, deep bur - ied in the
souls will soon a - wak - en, through Christ as - sured re -

1. lease, From
earth, Our
2. cease. This cru - el world to ban - ish, would
birth, With God in ra - diant glo - ry, from

be a bless - ed boon. I sigh for joys e -
care for - ev - er free, In heav'n - ly joy and

ter - nal; O Je - sus, Lord, come soon!
rap - ture. What fear has death for me?

Christoph Knoll, 1599

178

162
Herzlich thut mich verlangen
My Heart Is Ever Yearning

Matthäus-Passion

St. Matthew Passion

Hans Leo Hassler, 1601

B. A. 4, 214

O
Thou

Head, all scarred and bleed - ing, and heaped with cru - el
Head so filled with sor - row, and bound with crown of
coun - ten - ance so no - ble, yet now so pale and
all the world should hon - or, now foul - ly spat up

1. & 3.
scorn! O
wan, Which

2. & 4.
thorn! O
on! No

Head, that was so hon - ored, so
more Thine eyes are shin - ing, that

love - ly fair to see, And now so low de -
once did shine so bright; Ill us - age and ma -

grad - ed! My heart goes out to Thee!
lin - ing, af - flic - tion, shame and spite!

P. Gerhardt, 1656

179

163

Herzlich thut mich verlangen
My Heart Is Ever Yearning

Matthäus-Passion

St. Matthew Passion

Hans Leo Hassler, 1601   B. A. 4, 51 and 53

P. Gerhardt, 1656

164
Herzlich thut mich verlangen
My Heart Is Ever Yearning

Matthäus-Passion
St. Matthew Passion

B. A. 4, 248

Hans Leo Hassler, 1601

When comes my hour of part - ing, do not Thou part from me.
death's dread hour ap - proach - es, be - side me Thou wilt be.

me. As be. And when in aw - ful an - guish, my

time of death is nigh, Thy Cross will then up -

hold me, that stead - fast I may die.

P. Gerhardt, 1656

181

165

Herzlich thut mich verlangen
My Heart Is Ever Yearning

Weihnachts-Oratorium
Christmas Oratorio

Hans Leo Hassler, 1601

B. A. 5 II, 36

How can I right - ly greet Thee, how fit - ting - ly ex -
com - ing, Best Be - lov - ed, the Trea - sure of my

tol Thy soul? O Lord, I pray Thee car - ry the

torch to light my way, That I may know Thy

plea - sure, and serve Thee day by day.

P. Gerhart, 1653

166
Herzliebster Jesu, was hast du verbrochen
Dearest Jesus, What Wrong Hast Thou Done

Matthäus-Passion

St. Matthew Passion

B. A. 4, 23

Joh. Crüger, 1640

Ah, Je - sus dear,— what pre - cept hast Thou bro - ken, that such a cru - el— judge - ment has— been spo - ken? Where was Thy guilt, what— ev - il course pur - su - ing, or what wrong - do - ing?

Joh. Heermann, 1630

183

167

Herzliebster Jesu, was hast du verbrochen
Dearest Jesus, What Wrong Hast Thou Done

Matthäus-Passion

St. Matthew Passion

Joh. Crüger, 1640

B. A. 4, 192

How strange, how won - drous strange this cru - ci -
fix - tion; the Shep-herd for His sheep must bear af -
flic - tion. The Good King pays His sub - jects' ob - li -
ga - tion, de - spite His sta - tion.

Joh. Heermann, 1630

168

Herzliebster Jesu, was hast du verbrochen
Dearest Jesus, What Wrong Hast Thou Done

Johannes-Passion
St. John Passion

Joh. Crüger, 1640   B. A. 12 I, 17

Joh. Heermann, 1630

169

Herzliebster Jesu, was hast du verbrochen
Dearest Jesus, What Wrong Hast Thou Done

Johannes-Passion
St. John Passion

Joh. Crüger, 1640   B. A. 5, 52

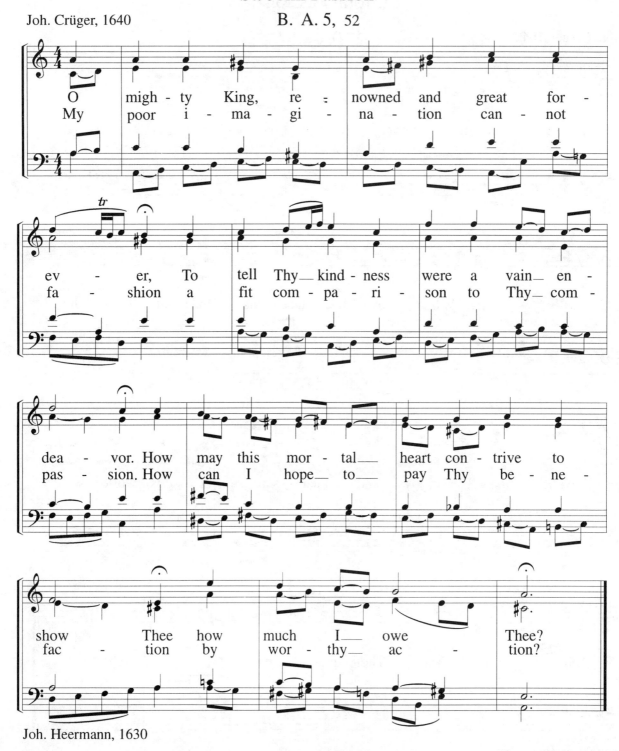

O mighty King, re - nowned and great for -
My poor i - ma - gi - na - tion can - not

ev - er, To tell Thy kind - ness were a vain en -
fa - shion a fit com - pa - ri - son to Thy com -

dea - vor. How may this mor - tal heart con - trive to
pas - sion. How can I hope to pay Thy be - ne -

show Thee how much I owe Thee?
fac - tion by wor - thy ac - tion?

Joh. Heermann, 1630

186

170

Heut' ist, o Mensch, ein grosser
This Day, O Man, Is One Of Bitter Pain

B. A. 39, N° 88

M. Apelles v. Löwenstern, 1644

This day, O man, is one of bit - ter pain; This
This day my God, my God has died for me. Yes,
Come! up, my soul, and get you to the Cross, To

day thy Sa - viour suf - fered and was slain, And
life it - self was hanged on Cal - va - ry. Can
hear, if may be, what could be the cause, And

ev - en down in death it - self has lain.
an - y - one be - lieve that this could be?
pen i - tent and griev - ing there to pause.

A. v. Löwenstern, 1644

187

171

Heut' triumphiret Gottes Sohn
Today God's Son Triumphs

B. A. 39, N° 89

Bartholomäus Gesius, 1601

Je - sus tri - um - phant rose to - day. Son He of God,_ who
life - less lay. Hal - le - lu - jah,_ hal - le - lu - jah!
Glo - ry and Might will He re - store. So thank we Him_ for
ev - er more. Hal - le - lu - jah, hal - le - lu - jah!

Basilius Förtsch, 1601

172

Hilf, Gott, dass mir's gelinge
Lord, Prosper My Endeavor

B. A. 39, N° 90

Praxis Pietatis, 1653

Heinrich Müller von Züthpen, before 1531

173

Hilf, Herr Jesu, lass gelingen
Help, Lord Jesus, That I Prosper

J. Schop, 1642

B. A. 39, N° 91

Help me, Je - sus, that I pros - per, all through-out this com - ing year. Give me va - lor, vim and vi - gor, hope and will to per - se - vere. Add - ed strength and cou - rage lend me; bless - ings new in mer - cy send me.

Joh. Rist, 1642

174

Ich bin ja, Herr, in deiner Macht
I Am Indeed, Lord, In Thy Power

B. A. 39, N° 92

J. S. Bach ?

Tis well with me for by Thy Might, Thou
coun-test well for the days and years, still

me to see
in this Vale

ma-kest me to see the light, to Thee my life it-self is
left me in to this Vale of Tears, and when from here I must be

1. ow - ing. Thou
2. go - ing. How, when and where I am

to die,
am to die, Thou know-est, Fa-ther, more than I

Simon Dach, before 1648

191

175

Ich dank' dir, Gott, für all' Wohlthat
I Thank Thee, God, For All Blessings

Cyr. Spangenberg, 1586
Eisleben G. B. 1598

B. A. 39, N° 93

With one ac - cord we thank Thee, Lord, for all the bless-ings

Thou af - ford. Lend me Thy Might, through all the

night; And this I pray, my Rock and Stay: From mi - se - ry keep

days not come to

Thou me free; let ev - il days not come to me.

J. Freder, 1552

T & B: days not come to me.

176

Ich dank' dir, lieber Herre
I Thank Thee, Dear God

J. K. Horn, 1544
Praxis pietatis, 1662

B. A. 39, N° 94

We thank Thee, Lord, for send-ing a-
Thou hast safe a-vert-ed the

gain the morn-ing light,That
dan-gers of _____

1. ing light,That

2. the night.With dark-ness deep a-

round us, we lay in dead-ly fear; But foes could not con-

found _____ us, for Thou, our God, _____ wert near.

Joh. Kolrose, 1535

177

Ich dank' dir, lieber Herre
I Thank Thee, Dear God

J. K. Horn, 1544
Praxis pietatis, 1662

B. A. 39, N° 95

We thank Thee, Lord, for send - ing a - gain the morn -
vert - ed the dan - gers of ____

1.
ing light, That Thou hast safe a - - the night; With

2.
dark - ness deep a - round us, we lay in dead - ly fear; But

foes could not con - found us, for Thou, our God, ____ wert near.

Joh. Kolrose, 1535

178

Ich dank' dir, lieber Herre
I Thank Thee, Dear God

Cantata 37. Wer da glaubet und getauft wird

He Who Believes And Will Be Baptised

J. K. Horn, 1544
Praxis pietatis, 1662

B. A. 7, 282

Con - fer Thou faith up - on me in Je - sus Christ

Thy Son; And grant me now the par - don, that He for me

has won. Thou wilt not now de - ny me, that

which Thou didst a - gree; From sin to pu - ri - fy me, and

lift its load from me.

Joh. Kolrose, 1535

179

Ich dank' dir schon durch deinen Sohn
I Thank Thee Through thy Son

B. A. 39, N° 96.

Michael Prætorius, 1610

Thank we Thee, Lord,____ that Thou af - ford

boun - ty and kind af - fec - tion;

That through_the night we have____ Thy Might,

rest - ing in Thy pro - tec - tion.

Zach. Berwaldt G. B., Leipzig, 1582

180

Ich danke dir, o Gott, in deinem Throne
I Thank Thee, O God, In Thy Throne

French Psalms, Geneva, 1551   B.A. 39, N° 97

O God, en-throned in Hea-ven High in splen-dor, through
Thy dear Son our thanks to Thee, we ren - der, That in our dan-ger
Thou dost not ne - glect us, But through the night from ev-'ry harm pro-
tect us. So har-ken, Lord, to this our sup-pli - ca - tion, And
keep us free from sin and tri-bu - la - tion.

Joh. Krüger G. B. 1640

181
Ich freue mich in dir
I Rejoice In Thee

Cantata 133. Ich freue mich in dir
I Rejoice In Thee

B. A. 28, 80

Joh. Balth. König, 1738

Melody not authenticated before Bach

My joy is all in Thee, and glad - ly will I
dear - rest Je - sus mine! As bro - ther may I
I cleave, O Lord, to Thee, though earth and sky be
all the u - ni - verse in thou - sand pie - ces

1. & 3.
greet Thee, Thou
shat - tered, And

2. & 4.
treat Thee! Of blood the same as Thine. Ah,
scat - tered. Thou, Je sus, Thou a - lone, art

word of sweet - est sound! What bless - ings rich and
all the world to me; Naught else I care to

rare, through Christ, the Lord, a - bound.
own, if I have on - ly Thee.

Caspar Ziegler, 1648

198

182

Ich hab' mein' Sach' Gott heimgestellt
I Have Left All My Belongings To God

Cassel G. B., 1601

B. A. 39, N° 38

My all to God do I sub-mit, to do with mine as
He sees fit. How-ev-er long my life may be, I
am con-tent that God's di-rec-tion go-vern me.

Joh. Leon c. 1329

183
Ich ruf' zu dir, Herr Jesu Christ
I Call To Thee, Lord Jesus Christ

Cantata 177. Ich ruf' zu dir, Herr Jesu Christ
I Call To Thee, Lord Jesus Christ

B. A. 35, 234

Jos. Klug G. B., 1535

I cry to_ Thee, Lord_ Je-sus Christ, and_ would. Thy_ pi-ty
To stow Thy_ grace up-on_ me now, nor_ let_ me_ be for-
Thou my_ weak-ness,_ Thou_ a-lone, can stay_ and make me_

1. & 3.
wa-ken; Be-
long-er; Help

2. & 4.
sa-ken; For I en-dea-vor,_
strong-er. A-gainst temp-ta-tion

Lord,_ in-deed, to live as Thou would_ have me. Faith-ful ev-
guard me, Lord, nor let it fur-ther_ hound me. All a-round

er, to serve my neigh-bor's need; To Thy Com-mand-ments_ loy-al.
me I see the hos-tile horde. Ah, let them not_ con-found_ me.

Joh. Agricola before 1530

184

Ich ruf' zu dir, Herr Jesu Christ
I Call To Thee, Lord Jesus Christ

Cantata 185. Barmherziges Herze der ewigen Liebe
Merciful Heart Of Eternal Love

Jos. Klug, 1535

B. A. 37, 118

Joh. Agricola before 1530

185

Jesu, der du meine Seele
Jesus, Thou My Soul

B. A. 39, N° 99

Praxis pietatis, 1682

Je - sus, by Thy Cross and Pas - sion, by the bit - ter
When the ev - il one would hold me, deep in Hell to

pain Thou bore. Migh - ti - ly a - way Thou bore me,
suf - fer sore,

with a Ha - ven Safe be - fore me. Through Thy Word, con -

tent - ment sweet. Thou art still my sure re - treat.

Joh. Rist, 1647

186

Jesu, der du meine Seele
Jesus, Thou My Soul

B. A. 39, N° 100

Praxis pietatis, 1662

Je - sus, by Thy Cross and Pas - sion, by the
When the E - vil One would hold me, deep in

bit - ter pain Thou bore, Migh-ti - ly a - way Thou bore
Hell to suf - fer sore.

me, with a Ha - ven Safe be - fore me. Through Thy Word con -

tent - ment sweet, Thou art still my sure re - treat.

Joh. Rist, 1641

187

Jesu, der du meine Seele
Jesus, Thou My Soul

Praxis pietatis, 1662

B. A. 39, N° 101

Je - sus, by Thy Cross and Pas - sion, by the bit - ter
When the Ev - il One would hold me, deep in Hell to

pain Thou bore,
suf - fer sore,

Migh-ti - ly a - way Thou bore me,

with a Ha - ven safe be - fore me. Through Thy Word, con -

tent - ment sweet. Thou art still my sure re - treat.

Joh. Rist, 1641

188

Jesu, der du meine Seele
Jesus, Thou My Soul

Cantata 78. Jesu, der du meine Seele

Jesus, Thou My Soul

Praxis pietatis, 1662

B. A. 18, 286

Lord, I trust Thee, I a-dore Thee, help my weak-ness, my de-spair;

Thou canst streng-then, Thou re-store me, when mis-deeds my faith im-pair.

On Thy lov-ing Grace re-ly-ing, God Al-migh-ty glo-ri-fy-ing,

By Thy side I hope to be ev-er through e-ter-ni-ty.

Joh. Rist, 1641

189

Jesu, der du selbst so wohl
Jesus, Thou Who Suffered So

Church and House Music
Breslau 1668 ?

B. A. 39, N° 102

Je-sus, Thou who suf-fered so, Thou who died to save me,

When it comes my time to go, let me meet death brave - ly.

When my faults I clear - ly see; When my sins as - sail me,

Let not Sa - tan van - quish me, nor my cour-age fail me.

Mich. Bapzien, c. 1656

190
Jesu, du mein liebstes Leben
Jesus, Thou My Dearest Life

B. A. 39, N° 103

Joh. Schop, 1642

Je - sus, light of my ex - is - tence,
Thou who suf - fered so to save me,

dear com - pan - ion of my soul.
Thou my heart's de - light and goal.

Je - sus, Thou my joy su - per - nal,
King and Shep - herd, Light E - ter - nal,

hope and Sa - viour, Trea - sure rare,
ah, how may I, worth - i - ly

my Re - deem - mer, Je - wel fair
ten - der thanks and praise to Thee?

Joh. Rist, 1642

191

Jesu, Jesu, du bist mein
Jesus, Jesus, Thou Art Mine

Probably by Bach
Schemelli G. B. 1736

B. A. 39, N° 104

Jesus, Jesus, Thou art mine, while the paths of earth I wander.

Let me, too, be wholly Thine, dear to Thee enthroned Yonder.

True to Thee, on Thee believing; When I die, to Thee fast cleaving.

All my being merged in Thine: Jesus, Jesus, Thou art mine.

Meiningen G. B. 1697

192

Jesu Leiden, Pein und Tod
Jesus Suffering, Pain And Death

Johannes-Passion

St. John Passion

B. A. 12 I, 39

Melch. Vulpius, 1609

Peter, while his con-science slept, thrice de-nied his Sa - viour.

When it woke he bit - ter wept, at his base be - hav - iour.

Je - sus, let me not for - get; true al - le - giance teach me.

When on e - vil I am set, through my con-sience reach me.

Paul Stockman, before 1636

193

Jesu Leiden, Pein und Tod
Jesus Suffering, Pain And Death

Johannes-Passion
St. John Passion

B. A. 12 I, 103

Melch. Vulpius, 1609

Of His moth-er, Christ took care, noth-ing He ne - glec - ted.

Bade the faith-ful ones pre - pare, that she be pro - tec - ted.

O Man, set - tle your af - fairs, that up - on the mor - row,

You may die re - leased from cares, free from grief and sor - row.

Paul Stockman, before 1636

194

Jesu Leiden, Pein und Tod
Jesus Suffering, Pain And Death

Cantata 159. Sehet, wir geh'n hinauf gen Jerusalem

Behold, We Are Going Up To Jerusalem

B. A. 32, 168

Melch. Vulpius, 1609

Je - sus' death in bit - ter pain, Je - sus' tri - bu - la - tion,
Je - sus, from Thy Pas - sion came all our hearts' e - la - tion,

Caused our mor - tal clay to gain heal-ing and sal - va - tion.
All Thy suf - fer - ing and shame were for our sal - va - tion.

mor - tal clay to gain
suf - fer-ing and shame

Chris- tians, put your cares a - way, leave your sins be - hind you,
So my spi - rit blos-soms forth, when I pause to pon - der

Ve - ri - ly will Judge-ment Day with the An - gels find you.
On the bliss-ful days to come, up in Hea - ven yon - der.

Paul Stockman, before 1636

195

Jesu, meine Freude
Jesus, My Joy

B. A. 39, N° 105

Joh. Crüger, Praxis pietatis, 1653

Je - sus, dear - est Mas - ter, Thou my spi - rit's Pas - tor,
Ah, how long in an - guish, must my heart thus lan - guish,

Shep-herd of my soul. Bea - con bright, my heart's de - light, far be-yond all
til it gains its goal?

earth - ly trea - sure, Thy re - gard I mea - sure.

Joh. Franck, 1653

196
Jesu, meine Freude
Jesus, My Joy

Motet: Jesu, meine Freude

Jesus, My Joy

Joh. Crüger, 1653

B. A. 39, 61 & 84

Je - sus, dear - est Mas - ter, Thou, my spi - rit's
Ah, how long in an - guish must my heart thus
Hence, thou imp of sor - row, joy comes with the
By my tri - bu - la - tion, gain I con - so -

Pas - tor, Shep - herd of my soul.
lan - guish, til it gains its goal?
mor - row; Je - sus is at hand.
la - tion; reach the Prom - ised Land.

Bea - con bright, my heart's de - light, Far be - yond all
With Thee near no harm I fear, Fear not death nor

earth - ly trea - sure, Thy re - gard I mea - sure.
fear dis - as - ter, Je - sus, dear - est Mas - ter.

Joh. Franck, 1653

197

Jesu, meine Freude
Jesus, My Joy

Cantata 81. Jesus schläft, was soll ich hoffen?
Jesus Is Sleeping, What Shall I Hope For?

Joh. Crüger, 1653   B. A. 20, I, 24

Un - der Thy pro - tec - tion, from the foe's sub -
Though the Fiend as - sail me, nor aught else a -

jec - tion, I am ev - er free.
vail me, Je - sus stands by me.

When in life the storm and strife, high with hell - ish

hor-rors heap me, Je - sus safe will keep me.

Joh. Franck, 1653

214

198

Jesu, meine Freude
Jesus, My Joy

Motet: Jesu, meine Freude
Jesus, My Joy

Joh. Crüger, 1653   B. A. 39, 66

Joh. Franck, 1653

199

Jesu, meine Freude
Jesus, My Joy

Motet: Jesu, meine Freude

Jesus, My Joy

Joh. Crüger, 1653

B. A. 39, 75

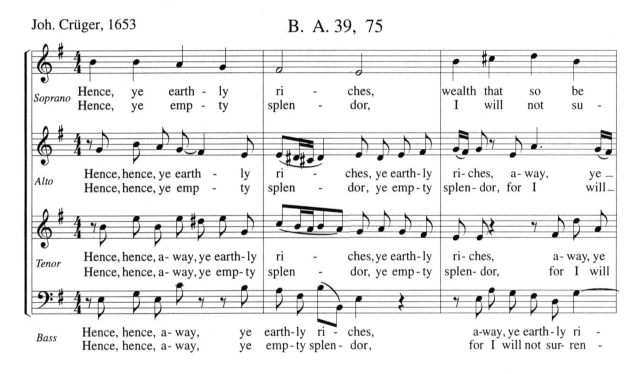

Soprano: Hence, ye earth-ly ri - ches, wealth that so be / Hence, ye emp-ty splen - dor, I will not su -

Alto: Hence, hence, ye earth - ly ri - ches, ye earth-ly ri - ches, a - way, ye _ / Hence, hence, ye emp - ty splen - dor, ye emp-ty splen- dor, for I will _

Tenor: Hence, hence, a- way, ye earth-ly ri - ches, ye earth-ly ri - ches, a - way, ye / Hence, hence, a- way, ye emp-ty splen - dor, ye emp-ty splen- dor, for I will

Bass: Hence, hence, a- way, ye earth-ly ri - ches, a-way, ye earth-ly ri - / Hence, hence, a- way, ye emp-ty splen- dor, for I will not sur- ren -

Soprano: wit - ches, Je - sus, Thee I crave. / ren - der, ne - ver be thy slave.

Alto: earth-ly ri - ches, Je - sus, Thee I crave, Thee I crave. / not sur-ren - der, ne - ver be thy slave, be thy slave.

Tenor: earth-ly ri - ches, Je - sus, Thee I crave. / not sur-ren - der, ne - ver be thy slave.

Bass: ches, Je - sus, Je - sus, Thee I crave, Thee I crave. / der, ne - ver, ne - ver be thy slave, be thy slave.

Death and pain do I dis - dain, Nor will a - ny

Death and pain do I dis - dain, death and pain dis- dain, nor

Death and pain do I dis - dain, death and pain dis -dain, nor will tri -

Death and pain do I dis - dain, nor will a - ny tri - al

tri - al grieve me, but that Je - sus leave me.

will tri - al grieve me, but that my Je - sus leave me.

al grieve me, but that my Je - sus leave me, my Je - sus leave me.

grieve me, but that my Lord, my Je - sus leave me.

Joh. Franck, 1653

200

Jesu, meine Freude
Jesus, My Joy

Cantata 64. Sehet welch' eine Liebe
See What A Love

Joh. Krüger, 1653   B. A. 16, 132

Fare thee well, thou plea - sure,   that we mor - tals
Fare thee well, wrong - do - ing,   ne - ver more a -

trea - sure;   thou art nought to me.
woo - ing   will I come to thee.

Fare thee well, thou emp - ty shell,   thine en - chant - ment

I must se - ver. Fare thee well for ev - er.

Joh. Franck, 1653

201
Jesu, meine Freude
Jesus, My Joy

Cantata 87. Bisher habt ihr nicht gebeten
Hitherto You Have Not Prayed

Joh. Crüger, 1653

B. A. 20   I, 152

Bless - ed is the spi - - rit, that has ev - er
Thou wilt warm em - brace it, at Thy side will
What is there to grieve me? Je - sus will not
Through His love I cap - ture Hea - ven's joy - ous

near it, Thee and love for Thee.
place it, from af - flic - tion free.
leave me, He will love me still.
rap - ture, con - quer ev - 'ry ill.

Thou our light and je - wel bright, Thou, the heart's most
For my grief He sends re - lief, Through His love the

pre - cious trea - sure, life and joy and plea - sure.
deep - est sad - ness chang - es in - to glad - ness.

Heinr. Müller, 1659

220

202

Jesu, meines Herzens Freud'
Jesus, Joy Of My Heart

Melody by J. R. Ahle
Joh. Flitner, 1661

B. A. 39, N° 108

Je - sus,_ Thou_ my hearts de-light, sweet-est_ Je -

sus. Thou,_ my_ joy_ will ev - er be, sweet - est_

Je - sus. Thou, my_ soul's se - cu - ri - ty,

sweet-est_ Je - sus, sweeet-est,_ sweet-est_ Je - sus.

Joh. Flitner, 1661

203

Jesu, nun sei gepreiset
Jesus, Now Be Praised

B. A. 39, N° 109

Christmas Songs: Wittenberg, 1591

Now join we all to praise Thee, this joy - ous New Year's
thank Thee that we meet here at this glad fes - tal

Day, For all the ma - ny bless - ings, that drive our cares a -
time, With gra - cious mer - cy la - den, and last - ing peace sub-

way. We   lime; That free and un - de - feat - ed, the

old year we com - plet - ed. To Thee in deep de - vo - tion, would

we_ be_ ev - er near. Pre - serve us, soul and bo - dy, through - out the com - ing_ year. In safe - ty watch and guard us, through all the com - ing_ year.

Joh. Hermann, Senior, 1591

204

Jesu, nun sei gepreiset
Jesus, Now Be Praised

Cant. 41. Jesu, nun sei gepreiset   B. A. 10, 58
Jesus, Now Be Praised

Cant. 171. Gott, wie dein Name   B. A. 35, 32 (in D major)
God, How Thy Name

Wittenberg, 1591

To Thee a - lone be glo - ry, to Thee a - lone be
til at last in Hea - ven, from care and trou - ble

3 trumpets

praise.
free,
In trou - ble teach us pa - tience, and
In peace and joy and glad - ness, we

kettledrums

gov - ern all our ways.
may be one with Thee.
Un -
Our

needs and ven - tures mea - sure ac - cord - ing to Thy plea - sure, And

so____ Thy peo - ple bring - ing to

Thee their faith sin - cere, With

trust - ing hearts are sing - ing: Bless

Thou this com - ing year,____ With trust - ing hearts are

sing - ing: Bless Thou this com - ing year.

Joh. Hermann, Senior, 1591

205

Jesu, nun sei gepreiset
Jesus, Now Be Praised

Cantata 190. Singet dem Herrn ein Neues Lied
Sing A New Song Unto The Lord

Wittenberg, 1591

B. A. 37, 257

Our
New year greet - ing | bring - ing, with | grate - ful hearts we
lives and mer - cy | spare us, Thy | faith - ful Chris - tian

come, Thy | praise and glo - ry | sing - ing, through-out all Christ - en -
band. Let | no mis - hap im - | pair us, and bless our Fa - ther -

1. dom. Our
2. land. Quell war and vain dis - | or - ders with - in our coun-try's

bor-ders. | Let truth and sim - ple | can - dor to | hon-or be re - stored.
Hy - po-cri-sy and | slan - der be | ev-'ry-where ab - horred.

Hy - po cri - sy and | slan - der be | ev-'ry-where ab - horred.

Joh. Hermann, Senior, 1591

206

Jesus Christus, unser Heiland
Jesus Christ, Our Saviour

B. A. 39, N° 1 10

Erfurt Enchiridion, 1524

Je - sus Christ, our Lord and Sa - viour,

turn, we pray God's an - ger from us.

Through the woe that Thee be - fell, pro -

tect us from the pains of hell.

Martin Luther, 1524

207

Jesus Christus, unser Heiland, der den Tod
Jesus Christ, Our Saviour, Who Death *

B. A. 39, N° 111

Jos. Klug, 1533

Je - sus Christ, our Lord and Sa - viour, is Vic - tor o - ver Death. He is_ a - ri - sen. Our sins has He im - pri - soned. Ky - rie e - le - i - son.

Martin Luther, 1524

* (Vanquished)

208

Jesus, meine Zuversicht
Jesus, My trust

B. A. 39, N° 112

Joh. Krüger, Praxis pietatis, 1653

Je - sus, Thou my comfort art, all through life my
Know - ing this, may not my heart, to my sorrows

firm re - li - ance. Though the night of
bid de - fi - ance,

death be near, dark with dread and fraught with fear?

Luise Henriette, Elector of Brandenburg (?) 1653

209

Jesus, meine Zuversicht
Jesus, My Trust

Cantata 145

So du mit deinem Munde bekennest Jesum
So Thou With Thine Own Tongue Confess To Jesus

B. A. 30, 95

Joh. Krüger, 1653

Up, my heart, this Glorious Day, gloomy fear from
Christ, the Lord, who lifeless lay, has from death to -

Man has driven; Comfort sure in
day arisen.

this we find: Jesus has redeemed mankind.

Caspar Neumann, around 1700

230

210

Ihr Gestirn', ihr hohlen Lüfte
Ye Stars, Ye Universe

B. A. 39, N° 1 13

Chr. Peter, 1655

All ye stars and winds of Hea - ven,
Deep ra - vines and lof - ty moun - tains,

thou the spa - cious fir - ma - ment,
hills and vales with e - choes rent.

(T.) with e - choes
(B.) with e - choes

Shout and sing in ex - ul - ta - tion,

cleave the clouds with ju - bi - la - tion.

Joh. Franck, 1655

211

In allen meinen Thaten
In All My Deeds

Joh. Quirsfeld, 1679
Gottfried Vopelius G. B., 1682

B. A. 39, N° 1 14

In all that I am do - ing, each en - ter - prise pur -

su - ing, I fol - low God's ad - vice; For

he who thus is heed - ing, is ev - er well suc -

ceed - ing, His ven - tures pay him thrice.

Paul Fleming, 1633

212

In dich hab' ich gehoffet, Herr
In Thee Have I Trusted, Lord

Cantata 52. Falsche Welt, dir trau ich nicht

False World, I Do Not Trust Thee

B. A. 12, II, 50

Sethus Calvesius, 1594

O Lord, as I have trust - ed Thee, from
have trust - ed

sin and shame keep Thou me free, nor let me

be con-found - ed. I pray to Thee, up-hold Thou
Grace sur - round - ed.

me, by Truth and Grace sur - round - ed.

Adam Reusner, 1594

213

In dich hab' ich gehoffet, Herr
In Thou Have I Trusted, Lord

Matthäus-Passion
St. Matthew Passion

B. A. 4, 151

Sethus Calvisius, 1591

The world, with trea - che - ry re - plete; with lies and fraud and false de - ceit, would tan - gle and en - snare me. Lord, keep, Thou me, from dan - ger free. From ev - il mal - ice spare me.

Adam Reusner, 1533

214

In dich hab' ich gehoffet, Herr
In Thou Have I Trusted, Lord

Weinachts Oratorium
Christmas Oratorio

B. A. 5 II, 190

Sethus Calvisius, 1594

Awake, ye souls,   this is the Day,   when
Thy splen-dor drives   the night a - way,   and

you may all be glad and gay, nor fret a - bout the
turns the dark - ness in - to day. Shed Thou Thy glo - ry

mor - row, God's Son was born this hap - py morn, in this
o'er   me. Thy beau-teous face and ra - diant grace, my

this sad Vale   of Sor - row.
light and guide   be - fore me.

Georg Weissel, 1642

sad Vale
and guide

215
In dulci jubilo
In Sweet Jubilation

B. A. 39, N° 115

Jos. Klug G. B., 1535

In dul-ci ju-bi-lo, sing we hap-py O-i-o.

Our de-light and glo-ry is ly-ing in the

man-ger, O. (T.) the man-ger He who is our sun-shine, was

born to Ma-ry long a-go. Al-pha He and He

O, O, Al-pha He and O.

14th or 15th Century

236

216
Ist Gott mein Schild und Helfersmann
Is God My Shield And Saviour

Cantata 58. Ich bin ein guter Hirt
I Am A Good Shepherd

B. A. 20 I, 118

Hundred Airs: Dresden, 1694

With God my shield and— su - re - ty, what
My Shep - herd True, with— Might - y Arm, pro -

can there be to in - jure me? I bid my— foes de -
tects me safe— from ev - 'ry harm, and foe— who— would as -

fi - ance. Ye, who with— guile my steps would— trace, will
sail me. They who would— give me grief or— pain, will

gain you no - thing— but dis - grace; For God— is— my re -
to their sor - row— strive in vain; For God— will— ne - ver—

li - ance, My God— is— my re - li - ance.
fail— me, My God— will— nev - er— fail— me.

Chr. Homburg, 1659

237

217

Keinen hat Gott verlassen
God Has No One Forsaken

B. A. 39, N° 116

Joh. Crüger, 1640

To them in God con-fid-ing, no__ ev-il can be-fall. The
wick-ed who de-ride Him, can__ harm Him not at all. The Lord pre-serves the
Faith-ful, and rais-es them on high; Pro-
vides our needs as mor-tals, and takes us__ when we die.

Erfurt G. B., 1611

218

Komm, Gott Schöpfer, heilger Geist
Come God Creator, Holy Ghost

B. A. 39, N° 117

Jos. Klug, 1535

Cre - a - tor, God and Ho - ly Ghost, Come,
en - ter, Thou, the heart of man. With Grace in - spire us
all to do what - ev - er Thou for us shall plan.

Martin Luther, 1524

219

Komm, Gott Schöpfer, heiliger Geist
Come God Creator, Holy Ghost

Cantata: Gott der Hoffnung erfülle euch

May The God Of Hope Fill You

B. A. 41, 238

Jos. Klug, 1535

Questionable authenticity

Martin Luther, 1524

220

Komm, heiliger Geist, Herre Gott
Come, Holy Ghost, Lord God

Cantata 59. Wer mich liebet   B. A. 12 II, 164

He Who Loves Me

Cantata 175. Er ruft seinen Schafen   B. A. 35, 177

He Calls His Sheep

Joh. Walther G. B., 1524

Come, Ho - ly ___ Ghost, help thou me to
Come, Ho - ly Spi - rit, come a - pace, and

seek Thee and to fol - low Thee. Thy Word my guide ___ and
fill us with Thy Sav - ing Grace. Give us cou - rage ___ that Thy

in - spi - ra - tion, To mould my life ___ for ___ my sal - va -
faith ___ im - parts. And with Thy love ___ en - flame our

tion. Thy Word a glo - rious morn - ing star, is shin - ing
hearts. The rays of Thy de - scend ing fire, all mor - tal

fair — from Hea-ven far. So firm — in faith — no doubt can
souls — with faith in - spire. The world a - round — with praise —

se - ver, I hold me true — to
ring - ing. A thou - sand tongues — Thy

God for - ev - er. Al - le - lu -
Name are sing - ing. Al - le - lu -

jah, al - le - lu - jah!
jah, al - le - lu - jah!

1st verse: J. Rist, 1651; 2nd verse: Martin Luther, 1524

221

Komm, heiliger Geist, Herre Gott
Come, Holy Ghost, Lord God

Motet: Der Geist hilft unsrer Schwachheit auf
The Spirit Helps Lift Our Weakness

B. A. 39, 16

Joh. Walther G. B., 1524

Thou fer - vor di - vine, com - fort sweet, make

Thou our peace and joy complete, that in Thy ser-vice naught can change

us, nor ev - il for - tune es-trange us. Lord,

streng-then us in time of stress, to fight our bo - dies' fee - ble-ness, and

brave - ly strive,___ we___ be - seech___ Thee, through
death and life___ at___ last to reach___ Thee. Al -
le - lu - jah, Al - le - lu - jah!

Martin Luther, 1524

222

Komm, Jesu, komm
Come, Jesus, Come

Motet: Komm, Jesu, Komm
Come, Jesus, Come

B. A. 39, 57

Come, Je - sus come, my limbs are wea - ry,
Glad - ly I clasp Thy hand ex - tend - ed,

my strength is gone, yea, more and more.
joy ful - ly bid this world fare - well.

I long for peace, and yearn for com - fort;
Has - ten, when life on earth is end - ed;

my drea - ry life is hard and sore.
there where my soul in peace may dwell.

Come, come, that I my all may give Thee.
Ev - er may dwell with my Cre - a - tor,

Thou art my Way of Life, the Path - way
with my Re - deem - er, Je - sus Christ, my

my Re-deem - er

to Sal - va - tion, Sal-va - tion
Li - be - ra - tor.

Wagner's G. B., Leipzig 1697. Book VIII, P. 326, with the note: John 14 v. 6. In its own melody.

223

Kommt her zu mir, spricht Gottes Sohn
Come Here To Me, Says God's Son

Cantata 74. Wer mich liebet, der wird mein Wort halten
He Who Loves Me, Will Trust My Word

B. A. 18, 146

Single sheet, 1530

Our   Fa - ther,   send   Thou   us   to - day   Thy   Ho - ly   Spi - rit
No   child   of   man   here   on   the   earth   is   ev - er   of   sud -

when   we   pray,   as   Thy   dear   Son   com - mand - ed.   Our
fic - ient   worth   to   gain   his   own   sal - va - tion.   But

pray'r   He   taught   us,   He   a - lone.   Let   us   not,   then,   Lord,
Je - sus   came   and   paid   the   price,   and   made   His   lov - ing

from   Thy   Throne   be   sent   back   emp - ty - hand - ed.
sac - ri - fice   for   us   in   ex - pi - a - tion.

Paul Gerhardt, 1636

224

Kommt her zu mir, spricht Gottes Sohn
Come Here To Me, Says God's Son

Cantata 108. Es ist euch gut, dass ich hingehe
It Is Good For You That I Go Away

B. A. 23, 230

Single sheet, 1530

Thy Spi-rit, sent from Heav'n a-bove, will lead our souls who know His love, in paths of con - se - cra - tion. He wise-ly guides our err - ing feet, when we are weak and in-dis-creet, and pe-ril our sal-va-tion.

Paul Gerhardt, 1656

225

Kyrie, Gott Vater in Ewigkeit
Kyrie, God The Father In Eternity

B. A. 39, N° 118

Dresden, 1625

our___ Hope___ and___ our Joy! Thou who hast re-

deemed us all from sin. Je - sus, Son of

God, Me - di - a - tor. To Thee en - throned on

high, we Thy ser - vants from our hearts be - seech

Thee! E - le - i - son.

Kyrie! O God, Holy Ghost! Keep us firm of faith and true to Thee. And when at last we die, joyful let us leave this Vale of Sorrow! Eleison.

Wittenberg, c. 1541

226

Lass, o Herr, dein Ohr sich neigen
Turn, O Lord, Thy Ear To Hear Me

B. A. 39, N° 119

Lyon, Bourgeoys,1547

Turn, O Lord, Thine ear to hear me. Drive me not from Thee a-
Heart-en by Thy Word and cheer me.

way, filled with an-guish and dis - may. Guard the soul that Thou cre-

a - ted, Which to thee is con - se - cra - ted. Help Thy

ser - vant, help Thou me. Lord, my hope is all in Thee.

Martin Opitz, 1637

227

Liebster Gott, wann werd' ich sterben
Dear God, When Will I Die

Cantata 8. Liebster Gott, wann werd' ich sterben
Dear God, When Will I Die

B. A. 1, 241

Daniel Vetter, before 1695

Caspar Neumann, c. 1690

253

228

Liebster Jesu, wir sind hier
Dearest Jesus, We Are Here

B. A.39, N° 120

Darmstadt G. B. 1687

Tob. Clausnitzer, 1668

229

Liebster Immanuel, Herzog der Frommen
Dearest Immanuel, Lord Of The Faithful

Cantata 123. Liebster Immanuel
Dearest Immanuel

B. A. 26, 60

A. Fritzsch, 1697

Dear-est Im - ma - nu-el, Lord of the Faith - ful,
Thou art my heart's de-light, Thou doth pos - sess it,
Get you gone, van - i - ty, cease you to cheat me.
Glad - ly I leave the world, soon Thou wilt greet me,

come Thou with me to dwell, Sa - viour di - vine!
glow-ing with love for Thee, yearn - ing for Thine.
Thou, Je - sus, Thou art mine, Thine on - ly I.
dwell deep with - in my heart, there when I die.

The 2nd time piano

Earth's fu - tile trea - sure gives me no plea - sure,
Thou art my Be - ing, my life de - cree - ing,

Thou art my heart's de - sire, O Sa - viour mine!
'til in the grave at last one day I lie.

A. Fritzsch, 1670

255

230

Lobe den Herren, den mächtigen König der Ehren
Praise The Lord, The Mighty King Of The Honorable

Cantata 137. Lobe den Herren, den mächtigen König
Praise the Lord, The Mighty King (B.A. 28,196)

and unfinished Wedding Cantata:

Herr Gott, Beherscher
Lord God, Ruler (B.A. 41,174)

Stralsund G. B. 1685

1. Praise God Al - migh - ty, our
It is a good - ly thing,
2. Praise God Al - migh - ty, whose
Who from His Hea - ven with
3. Praise ye Al - migh - ty God,
All breath - ing crea - tures for

King and our Rul - er ex - alt - ed.
prais - es to sing to the High - est.
boun - ty so rich - ly has blessed us.
show - ers of love has re - freshed us.
re - ve - rent bow ye be - fore Him!
grace and for mer - cy im - plore Him.

1. Strike strong the strings, psal - ter and harp to His
2. Pon - der ye thus, how migh-ty God aid - eth
3. He is the Light, come all ye faith - ful, u -

praise, Mu - sic and songs of thanks - giv - ing.
us, Think how and His love has pos - sessed us.
nite, wor - ship Him, praise and a - dore Him.

Joachim Neander, 1676

256

231

Lobe den Herren, den mächtigen König der Ehren
Praise The Lord, The Mighty King Of The Honorable

Cantata 57. Seelig ist der Mann
Happy Is The Man

B.A. 12 II,132

Stralsund G. B. 1665

Soul: Why hast Thou hid - den Thee, Je - sus,___ and___
All through the night have my thoughts un - to___
Jesus: Know thou, be - lov - ed one, naught will I___
Friend of thy soul, will I ev - er___ and___

left me ne - glec - ted?
Thee been di - rec - ted.
ev - er de - ny thee.
al - ways be nigh thee.

Why dost_ Thou_ still, sweet - est one, treat me_ so___
Well Thee_ I___ love, come then to Hea - ven_ a -

ill? Leave me for - lorn and ne - glec - ted?
bove. There will thy God glo - ri - fy Thee.

Saubert G. B., Nürnberg, 1676

232

Lobet denn Herren, denn er ist sehr freundlich
Praise The Lord, For He Is Very Friendly

B. A. 39, N° 121

A. Scandellus, 1568

Praise ye the Lord God, praise ye the Lord God, for His lov-ing kind - ness. How good and pleas - ing, all to sing God's prais - es, Chris-tian folk to - ge - ther. His prais-es to our ears are love-ly mu - sic. So praise the Lord God, praise ye the Lord God.

1579

258

233

Lobt Gott, ihr Christen allzugleich
Praise God, Ye Christians, All Together

B. A. 39. N° 122

Nic. Hermann, 1560 (1544)

Praise God en-throned a - bove the_ sky, ye Chris - tians, ev - 'ry one. This day He sent_ from_ Hea - ven High, His well - be - lov - ed Son,_____ His well - be - lov - ed Son.

Nic. Hermann, 1560

234

Lobt Gott, ihr Christen allzugleich
Praise God, Ye Christians All Together

B. A. 39, N° 123

Nic. Hermann, 1564

From out His Fa - ther's heart He came to hum - ble sta - ble

stall, A lit - tle child of fee - ble frame, yet Sa - viour of us

all, the Sa - viour of us all.

Nic. Hermann, 1560

235

Lobt Gott, ihr Christen allzugleich
Praise God, Ye Christians All Together

Cantata 151. Süsser Trost, mein Jesus kommt
Sweet Consolation, My Jesus Comes

B. A. 32, 16

Nic. Hermann, 1560 (1554)

The door of Heav'n He o-pened wide, on Pa-ra-dise we gaze. The guard-ian An-gel stands a-side, to God, the Lord be praise, to God, our Lord be praise.

Nic. Hermann, 1560

236

Lobt Gott, ihr Christen allzugleich
Praise God, Ye Christians All Together

Trauungs-Cantate: Dem Gerechten muss das Licht

Wedding Cantata: To The Righteous Must The Light

B. A. 13, I, 70

Nic. Hermann, 1560 (1554)

P. Gerhardt, 1648

237

Mach's mit mir, Gott, nach deiner Güt'
Do With Me, God, According To Thy Goodness

B. A. 39, N° 124

J. H. Schein, 1628

Thy bounty, Lord, deny me not, but pity my affliction. In diction. But take me, Lord, with Thee to dwell, for all is well that endeth well.

death let me not be forgot, nor lack Thy bene-

J. H. Schein, 1628

238

Mach's mir mir, Gott, nach deiner Güt'
Do With Me, God, According To Thy Will

Cantata 139. Wohl dem der sich auf seinem Gott
'Tis Well With Him Who On His God

B. A. 28, 248

J. H. Schein, 1628

'Tis___ well with him who on the Lord doth place his full re-
Hence-forth I flaunt the fiends of Hell, I fear not now death's

he may bid to Sa - tan's horde, and all the world de-
forth I sins of earth! I bid fare - well to all my faults and

1. & 3.

li - ance, For - fi - ance. True hap - pi - ness will
ter - rors. Out er - rors. In God I trust when

2. & 4.

him at - tend, who has in God__ a faith - ful friend
ills im - pend. Blest he whom God__ doth call His friend.

J. C. Ruben, 1692

239

Mach's mir, Gott, nach deiner Güt'
Do With Me, Lord, According To Thy Goodness

Johannes-Passion
St. John Passion

B. A. 12, I, 74

J. H Schein, 1628

Our freedom, Son of God, a-rose, when Thou wert cast in
from the dur-ance that Thou chose, our li-ber-ty is

pri - son. And ri - sen. Didst Thou not choose a

slave to be, we all were slaves e-ter-nal-ly.

240

Mein' Augen schliess' ich jetzt
Now I Close My Eyes

B. A. 39, N° 125

Apelles von Löwenstern, 1644

With God's Name on my lips, my wea-ry eye - lids close. My bo-dy wea-ry too, is yearn-ing for re - pose. How know I, Lord, but I may ne-ver see the morn-ing, This ve-ry night may die with - out a word of warn - ing?

Apelles von Löwenstern, 1644

241

Meinen Jesum lass' ich nicht
I Do Not Leave My Jesus

B. A. 39, N° 126

Lüneburger G. B., 1686

Je - sus mine a - bides with me, ne - ver, ne - ver
In my heart of hearts is He. To my heart will

will I leave Him. Firm be - lieve and
I re - ceive Him.

know ye well, ev - er there will Je - sus dwell.

Breslau, around 1690

242

Meinen Jesum lass' ich nicht
I Do Not Leave My Jesus

B. A. 39, N° 127

Andr. Hammerschmidt, 1638

Je - sus ne - ver leave I Thee, since Thy life for
me was gi - ven. Thou to me will ev - er be fet - tered
fast and firm - ly ri - ven. Light of Life art
thou to me; Ne - ver, ne - ver leave I Thee.

Christian Keymann, 1638

243

Meinen Jesum lass' ich nicht
I Do Not Leave My Jesus

Cantata 70. Wachet, betet, seid bereit
Awake, Pray And Be Ready

B. A. 16, 368

Andr. Hammerschmidt, 1658

Not for Hea-ven or the world, is my wea-ry spi-rit___ yearn-ing. Je-sus pled with God for me, all His wrath to kind-ness___ turn-ing. From His judge-ment set me free; Je-sus mine I cling to Thee.

Christian Keymann, 1658

269

244

Meinen Jesum lass' ich nicht
I Do Not Leave My Jesus

Cantata 154. Mein liebster Jesus ist verloren
My Dearest Jesus Is Lost

B. A. 32, 82

Andr. Hammerschmidt, 1658

Je - sus, part Thou not from me, stay Thou ev - er close be - side me. Keep me near and dear to Thee, to the Liv - ing Wa - ters guide me. Bles - sed who with me can say: "Je - sus Christ have I al - way."

Christian Keymann, 1658

245

Meinen Jesum lass' ich nicht
I Do Not Leave My Jesus

Cantata 157. Ich lasse dich nicht, du segnest mich denn
I Do Not Leave Thee, Surely Thou Wilt Bless Me

B. A. 32, 82

Andr. Hammerschmidt, 1658

Je - sus, part Thou not from me, stay Thou ev - er close be - side me. Keep me near and dear to Thee, to the Liv - ing Wa - ters guide me. Bles - sed who with me can say; "Je - sus Christ have I al - way."

Christian Keymann, 1658

271

246

Meinen Jesum lass' ich nicht
I Do Not Leave My Jesus

Cantata 124. Meinen Jesum lass' ich nicht
I Do Not Leave My Jesus

B. A. 26, 82

Andr. Hammerschmidt, 1658

Je - sus, part Thou not from me, stay Thou ev - er close be - side me. Keep me near and dear to Thee, to the Liv - ing Wa - ters guide me. Bless - ed who with me can say: "Je - sus Christ have I al - way."

Christian Keymann, 1658

272

247

Meinen Jesum lass' ich nicht
I Do Not Leave My Jesus

Final chorale of the St. Matthew Passion in its original form.

B. A. 26, 82

Andr. Hammerschmidt, 1658

Je - sus, part Thou not from me, stay Thou ev - er

close be - side me. Keep me near and dear to

Thee, to the Liv-ing Wa-ters guide me. Bles-sed who with

me can say: "Je - sus Christ have I al - way."

Christian Keymann, 1658

248

Meines Lebens letzte Zeit
My Life's Last Moment

B. A. 39, N° 128

Psalmodia sacra. Gotha, 1726

Life is well-nigh done for me; all too soon will it for-sake me.

Soon from earth-ly van - i - ty si - lent death will come and take me.

Man can not with - stand it, for our life is God's do - na - tion. None may

add to its du - ra - tion or ex - pand it.

249

Mit Fried' und Freud' ich fahr' dahin
In Peace And Joy I Go My Way

B. A. 39, N° 129

J. Walther G. B., 1524

In peace and joy I go my way, in God con-fid - ing; His will with heart and soul o-bey, safe a - bid - ing. All is well with me to-day; I wait the blest here-af - ter. af - ter here-af - ter.

Martin Luther, 1524

250

Mit Fried' und Freud' ich fahr' dahin
In Peace And Joy I Go My Way

Cantata 83. Erfreute Zeit im neuen Bunde
Joyful Time In The New Testament

B. A. 20, I, 76

J. Walther G. B., 1542

For all Man-kind He is the Light. All____ Cre - a -
tion is guid-ed by His Bea - con
bright to sal - va - tion. Sa - viour of the
Faith-ful He; We kneel in____ a - do - ra - tion.

Martin Luther, 1542

251

Mit Fried' und Freud' ich fahr' dahin
In Peace And Joy I Go My Way

Cantata 125. Mit Fried' und Freud'
In Peace And Joy

B. A. 26, 110

J. Walther G. B., 1524

For all Man-kind He is the Light. All Cre - a -
tion is guid-ed by His Bea - con
Bright, to sal - va - tion. Sa - viour of the
Faith - ful He. We kneel in a - do - ra - tion.

Martin Luther, 1524

252

Mitten wir im Leben sind
In The Midst Of Life Are We

J. Walther, 1524

B. A. 39, Nº 130

Lord. O Ho - ly Lord, our___ God! O

Ho - ly Migh - ty God! Sa - viour, Source of all Com -

pas - sion! Thou God Ev - er more! Let us

not be van - quished by the bit - ter - ness of

Ky - rie e - lei - son.

Death. Ky - rie e - lei - son.

Martin Luther, 1524

279

253

Nicht so traurig, nicht so sehr
Not So Sadly, Not So Much

B. A. 39, N° 131

J. S. Bach

Fret not, soul, that God gives thee fame and wealth in scan - ty
round a - bout thou see oth - ers who are giv - en

store. Though a - more. God is all that thou re -

quire. Let Him be thy heart's de - sire.

P. Gerhardt, 1649

254

Nun bitten wir den heiligen Geist
Now We Beseech The Holy Ghost

B. A. 39, N° 132

J. Walther G. B., 1524

To Thee the Lord, our God, we now pray, firm of faith that we Thy will o - bey. When our ho - ur com - eth, be Thou be - side us; safe - ly to our Home in Hea - ven guide us. Ky - rie - e - e - leis!

Martin Luther, 1525

255

Nun bitten wir den heiligen Geist
Now We Beseech The Holy Ghost

Trauungs cantate: Gott ist unsre Zuversicht
Wedding Cantata: God Is Our Trust

B. A. 13. I, 128

J. Walther G. B., 1524

Thou pre-cious Love, shed o'er us Thy Grace, and grant that Thy teach-ings we em-brace; that we love our neigh-bors, and each his bro-ther, liv-ing peace-ful all with one an-oth-er. Ky-ri-e e-leis.

Martin Luther, 1524

256

Nun bitten wir den heiligen Geist
Now We Beseech The Holy Ghost

Cantata 169. Gott soll allein mein Herze haben

God Alone Shall Have My Heart

J. Walther, 1524

B. A. 33, 192

Martin Luther, 1524

257

Nun danket alle Gott
Now Thank We All Our God

B. A. 39, N° 133

Joh. Crüger, 1648

Now thank we all our God, with hearts and hands and
all His won-drous works, for-ev-er man re-

voi - ces. In
joi - ces. Who from our moth-er's arms, His

boun - ty doth be - stow. From child-hood on through

life, His count-less bless - ings grow.

Martin Rinckart, 1648

258

Nun danket alle Gott
Now Thank We All Our God

Trauungschoral
Wedding Chorale

B. A. 13 I, 149

Joh. Crüger, 1648

Martin Rinckart, 1648

259

Nun danket alle Gott
Now Thank We All Our Lord

Cantata 79. Gott, der Herr, ist Sonn' und Schild
God, The Lord Is Sun And Shield

B.A. 18, 149

Joh. Crüger, 1648

In

Who from our

moth-er's arms,

His

boun-ty doth be - stow.

287

From child-hood on through life,

His count-less bless-ings grow.

Martin Rinckart, 1648

260

Nun freut euch, Gottes Kinder all
Now Rejoice, All God's Children

B. A. 39, N° 134

Single sheet, 1546

Re - joice, God's chil - dren, through the sky, our
Lord as - cends to Hea - ven High. So shout and sing and
praise His Name, with joy - ous voice and loud ac - claim.

Erasmus Alberus, 1549

261

Nun freut euch, lieben Christen g'mein
Now Rejoice, Dear Christian Folk

B. A. 39, N° 135

Wittenberg, 1524

Now / mu - sic sweet and
dance and sing, ye / good - ly song, re -
Chris - tian throng, re -

joi - cing all sin - cere - ly, With
sound - ing loud and / clear - ly, For

all the won - ders God doth do, for all His be - ne -

fits to you, for which He paid so dear - ly.

Martin Luther, 1523

262

Nun freut euch, lieben Christen g'mein
Now Rejoice, Dear Christian Folk

Jos. Klug, 1535
Cassel G. B. 1601

B. A. 39, N° 54

The day of Judge-ment is at hand, God's
come to judge the good and bad, E -

Son, so long ex-pec - ted, Will
lec - ted and re - jec - ted. But

lit - tle laugh-ter will we hear, with fires of Hell so

ve - ry near, as Pe - ter had pre-dic - ted.

Barth Ringwald, 1582

263

Nun freut euch, lieben Christen g'mein
Now Rejoice, Dear Christian Folk

Weihnachts - Oratorium
Christmas Oratorio

B. A. 5 II, 245

I stand beside Thy cradle here, O
all that Thou hast given me, which

Jesus Child, to tender The
I to Thee sur-

1. ten der The
2. ren der. Take

Thou my spirit, take my soul, my heart and mind in

Thy control, and graciously receive them.

264

Nun komm, der Heiden Heiland
Now Comes The Saviour Of The Heathens

Cantata 36. Schwingt freudig euch empor
Joyously Ascend Upwards

B. A. 7, 258

Erfurt, 1524

Come,   Thou   Sa - viour   of__   Man - kind,
Praise   to   God   here   ev - 'ry - one;

Child_ Thou   of   a   Vir - gin   born.   Mor - tals   o - ver
God_ the   Fa - ther,   God   the   Son.   God   the   Ho - ly

all__   the   earth,   mar - vel   at   Thy   Ho - ly   Birth.
Ghost_ a - dore,   praise   them   now   for - ev - er - more.

Martin Luther, 1524

265

Nun komm, der Heiden Heiland
Now Come, Saviour Of The Heathens

Cantata 62. Nun komm, der Heiden Heiland
Now Come, Saviour Of The Heathens

B. A.16, 50

Erfurt, 1524

Praise to God here ev - 'ry - one.

God_ the Fa - ther, God the Son, God the Ho - ly

Ghost_ a - dore. Praise them now and ev - er - more.

Martin Luther, 1524

266

Nun lasst uns Gott, dem Herren
Now Let Us [Praise] God, The Lord

Cantata 165. O heil' ges Geist und Wasserbad
O Holy Ghost And Baptismal Font

B. A. 33, 104

Nic. Selneccer, 1587

Now praise and thank_ thy_ Ma - ker, to
Thy Word, Com - mun - ion,_ Sa - cra - ment, will

be the_ free_ par - ta - ker of all the boun - teous
ward off_ all_ dis - as - ter; our faith in Thee un -

bless - ing, thou art from Him pos - ses - ing.
sha - ken, di - rect Thou us, dear_ Mas - ter.

Ludw. Helmbold, 1575

295

267

Nun lasst uns Gott, dem Herren
Now Let Us [Praise] God, The Lord

Cantata 79. Gott, der Herr, ist Sonn' und Schild

God, The Lord, Is Sword And Shield

Nic. Selneccer, 1587   B. A. 18,   316

In pro - bi - ty main - tain us, in li - ber - ty sus - tain us, to praise Thy Name for - ev - er, through Je - sus Christ, our Sa - viour.

Ludw. Helmbold, 1575

268

Nun lasst uns Gott, dem Herren
Now Let Us [Praise] God, The Lord

Cantata 194. Höchsterwünschtes Freudenfest
Most Desired Festival Of Joy

B. A. 29, 138

Nic. Selneccer, 1587

Up, heart, and praise with sing - ing, the
Ap - prove, Lord, my en - dea - vor, Thy
In cha - ri - ty ex - cell - ing, make

Lord of all Cre - a - tion, whose
coun - cil give me ev - er; Thy
Thou my heart Thy dwell - ing; Thy

boun - ty gives the Faith - ful pro -
help and com - fort lend - ing, to
Word my spi - rit's lea - ven, un -

tec - tion and sal - va - tion.
bring a hap - py end - ing.
til I come to Hea - ven.

P. Gerhardt, 1648

269

Nun lob', mein' Seel', den Herren
My Soul, Now Praise The Lord

B. A. 39, N° 136

Joh. Kugelmann, 1540

Now bless the Lord, now bless— Him, my soul, bless thou His
Lord, thy God, con - fess— Him, His be - ne - fits to

Ho - ly Name. The thee. ac - claim. Who all— thy sins for - giv - eth, all

thy— dis - eas - es cures; whom thy spi - rit liv - eth, who grace to

thee as - sures; Thy mouth with plen - ty fill - eth, with cour - age fires— thy

breast. The Lord is just and righ - teous to all that are— op - pressed.

Joh. Gramann (Poliander), 1540

298

270

Nun lob', mein' Seel', den Herren
My Soul, Now Praise The Lord

Joh. Kugelmann, 1540

B. A. 39, N° 137

Now bless the Lord, now bless Him, my soul, bless
Lord, thy God, con - fess Him, His be - ne -

thou His Ho - ly Name. The
fits to thee ac -

claim. Who all thy

sins for - giv - eth, all thy dis - eas - es

cures; Through whom thy spi - rit liv - eth, who

grace to thee as - sures; Thy mouth with plen - ty fill - eth, with cour - age fires thy breast. The Lord is just and righ - teous, to all___ who are op - pressed

Joh. Gramann (Poliander), 1540

271

Nun lob', mein' Seel', den Herren
My Soul, Now Praise The Lord

Cantata 17. Wer dank opfert, der preiset mich
He Who Offers Thanks, Glorifies Me

Joh. Kugelmann, 1540 B. A. 2, 225

Like as a fa-ther pi - ties the chil - dren
Lord will help the fee - ble, who come to

whom he loves and rears, Our
Him with child - like

1. fears. He knows our

2. He knows our

fee - ble pow - ers; that we are all but

dust, Like grass and leaves and flow - ers, when

blows the win - try gust, They droop and fade and pe - rish, de - cay____ and dis-ap - pear. So are the lives we che - rish; our end is ev - er near.

Joh. Gramann (Poliander), 1540

272

Nun lob', mein' Seel', den Herren
My Soul, Now Praise The Lord

Cantata 29. Wir danken dir, Gott, wir danken dir
We Thank Thee, God, We Thank Thee

B. A. 5 I, 316

Joh. Kugelmann, 1540

heart and will and mind. Hold fast to Him for -

ev - er; so sing__ we all__ to -

day: A - men for this is our por -

tion, that naught__ can take__ a - way.

that_____ naught can take a - way.

Nürnberg G. B., 1644

273

Nun preiset alle Gottes Barmherzigkeit
Now All Praise God's Mercifulness

B. A. 39, N° 138

M. Apelles v. Löwenstern, 1644

God's praise-es sound-ing, all wor-thy Chris-tian Folk, voi-ces re-sound-ing, His mer-cy here in-voke. Gra-cious He bids you to His ta-ble. Praise ye His mer-cy, bound-less and sta-ble.

M. A. v. Löwenstern, 1644

274

Nun sich der Tag geendent hat
Now The Day Has Come To An End

Adam Krieger, 1667
Darmstadt G. B. 1698

B. A. 39, N° 143

A - gain the day is past and done, no
lon - ger shines the sun. The wea - ry ones a -
gain may sleep, and cease at last to weep.

Joh. Friedr. Herzog, 1670

275

O Ewigkeit, du Donnerwort
O Eternity, Thou Thunder-Word

B. A. 39, N° 144

Joh. Schop, 1642

E - ter - ni - ty, thou Thun-der - word! Thou___ Sword to pierce my
E - ter - ni - ty, thou Time-less Time, I___ know not in my
E - ter - ni - ty, thou Thun-der - word! Thou___ Sword to pierce my
E - ter - ni - ty, thou time-less time, I___ know not in my

ve - ry soul, be - gun, but ne - ver end - ing.
bit - ter grief where, where I may be - take me.
ve - ry soul, be - gun, but ne - ver end - ing.
bit - ter grief where, where I may be - take me.

So deep the woe with - in my heart, which
Ah, take Thou me, when Thou di - rect, to

speech - less fear and dread im - part.
dwell with Thee and Thine e - lect.

Joh. Rist, 1644

307

276

O Ewigkeit, du Donerwort
O Eternity, Thou Thunder-Word

Cantata 20. O Ewigkeit, du Donnerwort
O Eternity, Thou Thunder-Word

B. A. 2, 317 & 327

Joh. Schop, 1612

Eternal as is God on High, enthroned a-bove the
suffer endless heat and cold, star-va-tion, terror,
Eter-ni-ty, thou Thun-der-word, thou sword to pierce my
ter-ni-ty, thou Time-less Time, I know not, in my

clouds and sky, our woes are ne-ver ceas-ing. We
grief un-told, and a-go-nies in-
ve-ry soul, be-gun but ne-ver end-ing. E-
bit-ter grief where I may yet be-

creas-ing. As
take me, So

God for-ev-er-more shall be, our
deep the woe with-in my heart, which

pain will last e-ter-nal-ly.
speech-less fear and dread im-part.

Joh. Rist, 1644

277

O Gott, du Frommer Gott
O God, Thou Holy God

B. A. 39, N° 145
Unfinished Cantata: Ehre sei Gott in der Höhe
Glory To God On High
B. A. 41, 114

A. Fritzsch, 1679
Darmstadt G. B., 1698

O God, Thou Ho - ly God, Thou Fount of ev - 'ry
My joy is all in Thee, and glad - ly will I
I cleave, O Lord, to Thee, though earth and sky be

Bless — ing! With - out Thee naught is ours, From
greet — Thee, Thou dear - est Je - sus mine. As
shat - tered, And all the world should be in

Thee our all pos - sess — ing. Vouch - safe to me, I —
Bro - ther I may — treat — Thee, of blood the same as —
thou - sand pie - ces — scat - tered. Thou, Je - sus, Thou a -

pray, a bo - dy hale and — strong, a
mine. Ah, Word of sweet - est — sound! What
lone, art all the world to — me! Naught

con - science clean and clear, a heart — that — knows no wrong.
bless - ings rich and rare through Christ the — Lord a — bound.
else I care to own, if I — have — on - ly Thee.

Caspar Zeigler, 1648

309

278

O Gott, du Frommer Gott
O God, Thou Holy God

Cantata 45. Es ist dir gesagt, Mensch, was gut ist
It Has Been Told To Thee, Man, What Good Is

A. Fritzsch, 1678
Darmstadt G. B., 1698

B. A. 10, 186

Grant me to find the task for which my tal - ents fit me, With stea - dy strength to strive, that I may well ac - quit me. And when my work is done, that some-thing may re - main for men to use, that I shall not have lived in vain.

Joh. Heerman, 1630

279

O Gott, du Frommer Gott
O God, Thou Gentle God

Cantata 128. Auf Christi Himmelfahrt allein
For Christ Alone Ascension

A. Fritzsch, 1679
Darmstadt G. B., 1698

B. A. 26, 184

O Je-sus, my de-light, my spi-rit's be-ne-dic-tion, have
So wilt Thou al-so,— Lord, at Thy right hand then place— me, and

pi-ty on my— plight, and call me from af-flic-tion. When
as Thy par-doned— child, with lov-ing grace em-brace— me? What

shall I once be-free to come, dear Lord,— to— Thee, To
joy a-waits me— There, with Thee on High— to— be, Thy

cross the star-ry sky, to Thee in Hea-ven High?
Ma-jes-ty to share, through all E-ter-ni-ty!

Matthäus Habermann, 1673

280

O Gott, du frommer Gott
O God, Thou Holy God

Cantata 64. Sehet, welch' eine Liebe
See, What A Love

A. Fritzsch, 1679
Darmstadt G. B., 1698

B. A. 16, 120

What care I for the world, with all its pomp and plea-sure? My

joy is all in Thee, Thy love a-lone I trea-sure. Ap-

pro-val in Thy sight will be my one de-light. If

I am loved by Thee, what is the world to me?

Georg Michael Pfefferkorn, 1667

281

O Gott, du frommer Gott
O God, Thou Holy God

Cantata 64. Sehet welch' eine Liebe

See, What A Love

B. A. 16, 372

Cantata 94. Was frag' ich nach der welt

What Care I For the World

A. Fritzsch, 1679

Darmstadt G. B., 1698

B. A. 22, 127

What care I__ for the world, with all its pomp and
What care I__ for the world, whose ri - ches men so
What care I__ for the world, with Je - sus my De -

plea - sure? My joy is all in Thee, thy
che - rish? Its glo - ries, goods and gains, will
fen - der? My trea - sure and my life, to

love a - lone I__ trea - sure. Ap - pro - val in Thy
in an in - stant__ pe - rish. Its bick - er - ings and
Him I all sur - en - der. My chief - est joy on

sight,   will be   my   one   de -   light.   If
hate,   and all   its   van - i -   ty;   If
earth,   and hope of   Hea - ven   He;   So

I   am loved by   Thee,   what is   the world   to   me?
I   but keep the Faith,   what is   the world   to   me?
I   say once a - gain, what is   the world   to   me?

Georg Michael Pfefferkorn, 1667

282

O Gott, du frommer Gott
O God, Thou Gentle God

Meiningen G. B., 1693   B. A. 39, N° 146

O God, Thou Ho - ly God, Thou Fount of ev - 'ry
out Thee naught is ours. From Thee our all pos -

1. Bless - ing. With -
2. sess - ing. Vouch - safe to me, I

pray, a bo - dy hale and strong, A

con - science clean and clear, a heart that knows no wrong.

Joh. Heerman, 1630

315

283

O Herre Gott, dein göttlich Wort
O Lord God, Thy Godly Word

Cantata 184. Erwünschtes Freudenlicht
Desired Light Of Joy

Erfurt, 1527
Jos. Klug G. B., 1535

B. A. 37, 95

O Lord our God, Thy Ho-ly Word was long ob-scure and hid-
The by Thy Grace, what Thou hast said, by Paul was clear-ly writ-
out the strife of Migh-ty God will com-fort and pro-tect
mor-tal life, in love and faith di-rect

1. & 3.
den, 'Til me. Through-

2. & 4.
ten. me.
And af-ter Paul, Thy Teach-ers all, Thy
And when at last my time has passed, let

Say-ings well ex-pound-ed. So thank we Thee, Lord
not my spi-rit per-ish, But take Thou me to

God, that we may now not be con-found-ed.
dwell with Thee, my soul with Thee to cher-ish.

Erfurt G. B., 1527

316

284

O Herzenangst, o Bangigkeit und Zagen
O Heart's Distress, O Dread And Fear

B. A. 39, N° 147

Probably by J. S. Bach

Weary with woe, my heart is deep de-
heart is deep
spair-ing! What see I here? Whose bo-dy are
they bear -ing? Whose is the grave, the stone and the
name on it? For I should know Him!

Fr. D. Gerh. Müller von Königsberg

317

285

O Lamm Gottes, unschuldig
O Innocent Lamb Of God

Nic. Decius, 1531
Joh. Spangenberg G. B., 1545

B. A. 39, 148

O Lamb of God, un - spot - ted, yet cru - ci - fied and
rene and ev - er pa - tient, al - tho' de - spised and

butch - ered. Se - tor - tured. All sin for our sake

bear - ing, else would we die de - spair - ing. Have

pi - ty on us, O___ Je - sus!.

Nic. Decius, 1531

286

O Mensch, bewein' dein Sünde gross
O Man, Thy Grievous Sins Bemoan

Strassburg Psalms, 1526

B. A. 39, N° 149

Sebald Heyden, 1526

287

O Mensch, schau Jesum Christum an
O Man, Contemplate Jesus Christ

B. A. 39, N° 150

P. Titus, 1603

Mor - tal, re - mem - ber Je - sus Christ, and how He died for thee; How He, a God, be - came a man, from sin to set thee free. Ah, how sore my heart doth ache with an - guish for His sake.

J. Specht

320

288

O Traurigkeit, o Herzeleid
O Sadness, O Heartache

Joh. Rist, 1641

B. A. 39, N° 151

O woe— and grief past all be - lief! O ho - ur of de - spair - ing! God's own son, His Faith - ful Ones, to His grave are— bear - ing!

Joh. Rist, 1641

289

O Welt, ich muss dich lassen
O World, I Must Leave Thee

B. A. 39, N° 140

Georg Forster's Song Collection, 1539
Melody ascribed to Heinrich Isaak, c. 1490

O world, thy life— is end - ed, high— on the Cross sus -

pend - ed. To - day thy Sa - viour— died. The

Lord of all— cre - a - tion, in— shame and de - gra -

da - tion, was scourged, re - viled and cru - ci - fied.

P. Gerhardt, 1648

290

O Welt, ich muss dich lassen
O World, I Must Leave You

B. A. 39, N° 141

Georg Forster's Song Collection, 1539

O__ world, thy life__ is end - ed, high__ on the Cross sus - pend - ed. To - day thy Sa - viour__ died. The__ Lord of all__ cre - a - tion, in__ shame and de - gra - da - tion, was scourged, re - viled__ and__ cru - ci - fied.

P. Gerhardt, 1648

291

O Welt, ich muss dich lassen
O World, I Must Leave Thee

B. A. 39, N° 142

G. Forster, 1539

O world, thy life is end - ed, high on the Cross sus -
pend - ed. To - day thy Sa - viour died. The
Lord of all cre - a - tion, in shame and de - gra -
da - tion, was scourged, re - viled and cru - ci - fied.
Alto: and cru - ci - fied.

P. Gerhardt, 1648

292

O Welt, ich muss dich lassen
O World, I Must Leave Thee

Matthäus-Passion

St. Matthew Passion

B. A. 4, 164

G. Forster, 1539

Who was it, Lord,— did smite Thee, Thy— good with ill re-

quite Thee, so foul-ly treat-ed— Thee? For

Thou wert no— of - fen - der, nor— didst to sin sur-

ren - der. From e - vil Thou wert— ev - er free.

P. Gerhardt, 1648

293

O Welt, ich muss dich lassen
O World, I Must Leave You

Johannes-Passion (Nº 8)
St. John Passion

B. A. 12 I, 31

G. Forster, 1539

Who was it, Lord, did smite Thee, Thy good with ill re-
My sins and e - vil do - ing are like the sands be-

quite Thee, so foul - ly treat - ed Thee? For
strew - ing the migh - ty o - cean's shore. These

Thou wert no of - fen - der, nor didst to sin sur -
sins it was that brought Thee Thy mi - se - ry, and

ren - der. From e - vil Thou wert ev - er free.
wrought Thee the host of tor - ments that Thou bore.

P. Gerhardt, 1648

294

O Welt, ich muss dich lassen
O World, I Must Leave Thee

Matthäus-Passion (Nº 16)
St. Matthew Passion

B. A. 4, 42

G. Forster, 1539

'Tis I who should, re - pent - ing, in tor - ment un - re - lent - ing, en - dure the pains of Hell. The sha - ckles and the scour - ges, Thou bore from sin to purge us, were we de - serv - ing all too well.

P. Gerhardt, 1648

295

O Welt, ich muss dich lassen
O World, I Must Leave Thee

Cantata 13. Meine Seufzer, meine Thränen
My Sighs, My Tears

B. A. 2, 98

G. Forster, 1539

In all that I am do - ing, each en - ter - prise pur -
Be His, my soul_ for - ev - er, that_ naught from thee can

su - ing, I fol - low God's ad - vice. For
se - ver, Him who cre - at - ed_ thee. What -

he who this_ is heed - ing, is_ ev - er well suc -
ev - er ills_ as - sail thee, thy_ Fa - ther will not

ceed - ing; his ven - tures ev - er pay him thrice.
fail thee; thine ev - 'ry need will He for - see.

P. Fleming, 1633

296

O Welt, ich muss dich lassen
O World, I Must Leave Thee

Cantata 44. Sie werden euch in den Bann thun
You Shall Be Excommunicated

B. A. 10, 150

G. Forster, 1539

Be His, my soul for - e - ver, that naught from thee can

se - ver Him who cre - a - ted thee. What-

ev - er ills as - sail thee, thy Fa - ther will not

fail thee. Thy ev - 'ry need will He for - see.

P. Fleming, 1633

297

O welt, ich muss dich lassen
O World, I Must Leave Thee

Cantata 97. In allen meinen Thaten
In All My Deeds

B. A. 22, 230

G. Forster, 1539

Be His, my soul, for - e - ver, that naught from thee can

se - ver Him who cre - a - ted thee. What -

ev - er ills as - sail me, my Fa - ther will not

fail me, my ev - 'ry need for - see.

P. Fleming, 1633

298

O welt, ich muss dich lassen
O World, I Must Leave Thee

B. A. 39, N° 139

G. Forster, 1539

P. Gerhardt, 1648

299

O wie selig, seid ihr doch, ihr Frommen
O How Happy Are You Then, Ye Pious Folk

B. A. 39, N° 152

Joh. Crüger, 1649

Bless-ed ye who_ live in Faith un - swerv - ing, Ye_ who die the

Grace of_ God de - serv - ing! Through Hea - ven's

Por - tals you es - cape the chains that bind us mor - tals

Simon Dach, 1639

300

O wie selig seid ihr doch, ihr Frommen
O How Happy Are You Then, Ye Pious Folk

B. A. 39, N° 153

Böhm Brothers G. B., 1506

Bless-ed ye who live in Faith un-swerv - ing, Ye who die the Grace of God de - serv - ing. Through Hea-ven's Por - tals you es - cape the chains that bind us mor - tals.

Simon Dach, 1639

301

O wir armen Sünder
O We Poor Sinners

B. A. 39, N° 154

Lucas Lossius, 1561

Hermann Bonn, 1542

302

Puer natus in Bethlehem
A Child Is Born In Bethlehem

Cantata 65. Sie werden aus Saba alle kommen
You Shall All Come Out Of Sheba

B. A. 16, 152

Lucas Lossius, 1553 (1561)

From the 13th century

V. Babst G. B., 1545

303

Schaut, ihr Sünder
Look, Ye Sinners

B. A. 39, N° 155

M. A. v. Löwenstern, 1644

Christ speaks from the Cross

Look, ye sin - ners! Great woe you bring to me.

Ye, the off - spring of death would ev - er be.

My death freed you from mor - tal death's dis - tress.

It will speed you to joy and— bless - ed - ness.

M. A. v. Löwenstern, 1644

304

Schmücke dich, o liebe Seele
Bedeck Thyself, O Dear Soul

Cantata 180. Schmücke dich, o liebe Seele
Bedeck Thyself, O Dear Soul

B. A. 35, 322

Joh. Crüger, 1649

Deck thy - self, my soul with glad - ness; shun the
Come in ra - diance bright to ren - der hom - age
Je - sus, Bread of Life, sus - tain us; through Thy
By Thy Sav - ing Grace en - a - ble us to

haunts of sin and sad - ness At the feast of our sal - va -
to His might and splen - dor. Sa - cred sup - per,
love sal - va - tion gain us. soul re - gal -
ga - ther at Thy ta - ble.

tion, He has bid us take our sta - tion. He who high in
ing, keep our spi - rits ne - ver fail - ing; That we, while on

Hea - ven reign - eth, yet to dwell with mor - tals deign - eth.
earth so - journ - ing, be for Hea - ven ev - er yearn - ing.

Joh. Franck, 1649

305

Schwing' dich auf zu deinem Gott
Soar Up To Thy God

Cantata 40. Dazu ist erscheinen der Sohn Gottes
With This The Son Of God Is Come

Dan. Vetter, 1713
Somewhat changed by Bach

B. A. 7, 387

Up, my soul, and cease to plod, thus in gloom-y— fol - ly,
Shake you now your head and say: "Ser-pent, I ab - hor you!"

Mak-ing mock-er - y of God, by your mel - an - cho - ly.
Gone is now your ven - omed sting, noth-ing can re - store you.

Mark you not how Sa - tan's horde press-es hard up - on— you?
Comes the Sa - viour armed to slay; lops off all your bad - ness.

He would wreck the peace your Lord Je - sus Christ has won you.
Takes me with Him far a - way, to the Land of Glad - ness.

Paul Gerhardt, 1653

339

306

Seelenbräutigam
Holy Bridegroom

B. A. 39, N° 156

Darmstadt G B., 1698

Com - rade of my soul, Je - sus, Lamb of God,

ne - ver is Thy love de - nied me. Through the

mire of sin Thou guide me, where man - kind has

trod, Je - sus, Lamb of God!

Adam Drese, 1697

307

Sei gegrüsset, Jesu gütig
Be Thou Greeted, Benevolent Jesus

B. A. 39, N° 157

Gottfried Vopelius G. B., 1682

Thee I greet, Thy love I trea-sure, ten-der far be - yond all _ mea -

sure. Ah, how wert Thou mu - ti - la - ted, all Thy

bo - dy la - ce - ra - ted! Grant that I Thy

love in - her - it, when I die, Thy bless-ing _ mer - it.

Christian Keymann, before 1662

308

Singen wir aus Herzensgrund
We Sing From The Depths Of Our Heart

Cantata 187. Es wartet Alles auf dich
All Awaits Thee

B. A. 37, 191

G. B. of the Böhm Brothers, before 1544

Hear - ti - ly   sing - ing,   we re - joice;
God has pro - vi - ded   for us   all;
Thank - ful to   Thee,   with hope we   pray:

praise our   God   with joy - ous   voice.
food for   crea - tures   great and   small.
"Send Thou Thy   Spi - rit   here to - day.

All   His   crea - tures   He has   fed;
Grass   He   grows   on   hill and   dale,
Make   us   right - ly   un - der - stand

food   for   fish - es,   bird   and   beast;
lest   the   food for   cat - tle   fail;
how   to   fol - low   Thy   com - mand."

from the great - est to   the   least;
gives to mor - tals bread   and   wine;
True to Thee   through all   our   days,

giv - en man   his   dai - ly   bread;
rain for flow - er, tree   and   vine;
to Thy Name   with joy   we   raise

lov - ing   care   that ne - ver   ceased.
made for   man   by God's de - sign.
voi - ces   filled   with end - less   praise.

Frankfurt on the Oder, 1568

309

Singt dem Herrn ein neues Lied
Sing A New Song To The Lord

B. A. 39, N° 158

M. A. von Löwenstern, 1644

praise Him all the con - gre -

Sing to God a new - made song; praise Him all the
Let your song be fair and strong; peace we have through -

ga - tion.

con - gre ga - tion. So we praise our Mak - er e -
out our na - tion.

ver, He who dwells be - yond the skies; who in

need gives coun - sel wise, who for - gets His peo - ple ne - ver.

M. A. von Löwenstern

310

So giebst du nun, mein Jesu, gute Nacht
So Give Thou Now, My Jesus, A Good Night

B. A. 39, N° 159

Dresden, 1694

So must I say: "My Je - sus, fare Thee well!" Thou

wert my life, and_ I_ am bro - ken-heart-ed. Thy pain is done, and

all that Thee be-fell. My Lord is dead, His_ Spi - rit has de -

part - ed. My Lord is dead, His_ Spi - rit has de - part - ed.

Aug. Pfeifer, † 1698

311

Sollt' ich meinem Gott nicht singen
Shall I Not Sing Of My God

B. A. 39, N° 160

Jos. Schop, 1641

Shall I not ex - alt my Mak - er,
When I see in ev - 'ry quar - ter

sing to Him and thank-ful be,
all His be - ne - fits to me?

Love un - end - ing, pure and fer - vent,

moves the heart of God a - bove;

fills and a - ni - mates with love
him who is His faith - ful ser - vant.
Kings and King - doms fall and rise.
God's de - vo - tion ne - ver dies.

P. Gerhardt, 1656

312

Straf mich nicht in deinem Zorn
Do Not Punish Me In Thy Anger

Cantata 115. Mache dich, mein Geist, bereit
Prepare Thyself, My Spirit

Dresden, 1694

B. A. 24, 132

Come, my soul, thy - self pre - pare,
Do not let the trum - pet's blare
Bear we then our woes and cares,
Lest the Day come, un - a - ware,

watch - ing, pray - ing, plead - ing
find thee all un - heed - ing.
pe - ni tent and fear - ing;
which is ev - er near - ing.

Ah, be - ware Sa - tan's snare! Let him not dis -
Watch and pray comes the Day when the whole world

may___ thee, seek - ing to be - tray thee.
crash es in - to dust and ash - es.

Joh. Burchard Freystein, 1697

348

313

Uns ist ein Kindlein heut' gebor'n
Unto Us A Little Child Is Born Today

B. A. 39, N° 161

Barth. Gesius, 1601 (somewhat changed)

To us— up-on this hap-py morn, the Vir-gin Fair—
joi-ces all the An-gel Host; should not man-kind—

a Child has borne. Re—
be re-joi-cing most? With hear-ty thanks our

God a-dore, and praise His mer— cy more— and more.

In the Psalmodia of Luc. Lossius, 1579

314

Valet will ich dir geben
I Will Say Farewell To Thee

B. A. 39, N° 162

Melch. Teschner, 1613

To thee, thou world of e - vil, I
hard and faith - less fa - shions, are

glad - ly bid "Fare - well." Thy shell. To_ Hea - ven, hap - py
but an emp - ty

dwell - ing, 'tis there that I would go; Where

God_has called the Faith - ful, who serve Him here be - low.

Valerius Herberger, 1613

315

Valet will ich dir sagen
I Will Say Farewell To Thee

Johannes-Passion
St. John Passion

B. A. 12 I, 95

Melch. Teschner, 1613

With- in my heart's re- cess - es, there spar - kles bright Thy
heart of hearts re - joi - ces, to see its stead - y

Name! My flame. When- dread-ed death is near - ing, with

all its dark dis - tress, Thy Cross,— dear Lord, ap -

pear - ing, will ease its bit - ter - ness.

Valerius Herberger, 1613

316

Vater unser im Himmelreich
Our Father In Heaven

Johannes-Passion; 8. das Vorwort
St. John Passion - The Foreword

B. A. 39, N° 163 -12 I

Val . Schumann G. B., 1539

Our Fa - ther throned in Hea-ven High, to Thee in need Thy peo - ple cry; Thou who as bro - thers count us all, we pray Thee har - ken to our call. Teach us the prayer that Grace im - parts; Not from the lips but from the hearts.

Martin Luther, 1539

317

Vater unser im Himmelreich
Our Father In Heaven

Johannes-Passion
St. John Passion

B. A. 12 I, 18

Val. Schumann G. B. 1539

Thy will must all Cre - a - tion do, on earth and high in Hea - ven too; And pa - tience, Lord, on us be - stow, o - be - di - ent in weal and woe. Stay Thou the hand and spoil the skill of them who seek to thwart Thy will.

Martin Luther, 1539

318

Vater unser im Himmelreich
Our Father In Heaven

Cantata 101. Nimm von uns, Herr, du treuer Gott

Take From Us, Lord, Thou True God

B. A. 23, 32

Val. Schumann G. B., 1539

Have mer-cy, Lord, and hear our prayer, for-give our faults, Thine
Lord, lead us by Thy guid-ing hand, bless Thou our town and

an-ger spare. From sin, from en-vy and from pride, de-
na-tive land. Pre-serve to us Thy Ho-ly Word, a-

liv-er us, and be our guide. From war and strife keep
gainst the wiles of Sa-tan's Herd. Grant, Lord, a bless-ed

Thou us free; from plague and want and mi-se-ry.
death for me, and life E-ter-nal There with Thee.

Martin Moller, 1584

319

Vater unser im Himmelreich
Our Father In Heaven

Cantata 90. Es reifet euch ein schreklich Ende
A Terrible End Is Being Readied For You

B. A. 20 I, 214

Val. Schumann G.B., 1539

Lord, lead us by Thy Guid-ing Hand; bless Thou our town and na-tive land. Pre-serve to us Thy Ho - ly Word a - gainst the wiles of Sa - tan's Herd. Grant, Lord, a bless - ed death to me, and Life E - ter - nal There with Thee.

Martin Moller, 1584

320

Vater unser im Himmelreich
Our Father In Heaven

Cantata 102

Herr, deine Augen sehen nach dem Glauben

Lord, Thine Eyes Look Upon The Believers

B. A. 20 I, 214

Val. Schumann G. B., 1539

"Now as I live," the Lord God saith, "I val - ue not a
To - day a - live and in your prime, get you to God while
Help Thou, Lord Je - sus, help Thou me, that I to - day may

sin - ner's death, but bet - ter far am I con - tent that
there is time. To - day a - lert and sound and brave; to -
come to Thee; And teach, I pray Thee, pe - ne - tence, be -

from his sins he shall re - pent; From e - vil ways to
mor - row sick or in your grave. By pe - ne - tence God's
fore swift death shall bear me hence. That read - y I may

turn to me, and live with me e - ter - nal - ly."
wrath dis - pel, or face the fiend - ish fires of Hell.
ev - er be to take my jour - ney home to Thee.

Joh. Heermann, 1630

321

Verleih' uns Frieden gnädlich
Graciously Grant us Peace

Cantata 126. Erhalt' uns, Herr, bei deinem Wort
Sustain Us, Lord, By Thy Word

Nürnberg, 1531
Jos. Klug G. B., 1535

B. A. 26, 131

In gra-cious mer-cy__ grant us peace, O Lord, for life's du-ra-tion. We've none to help__ us should__ Thou cease to__ strive for our sal-va-tion. On Thee, our God,__ do we__ re-ly. In-sure us, through the rul-ers of our land, peace and good gov-ern-ment; That

un - der their com - mand, free from war and tur - moil we may live and pros - per, Up-right, pi - ous, re - ve - rent, fear-ing the Lord. A - men.

Martin Luther, 1531 and 1566

322

Verleih' uns Frieden gnädlich
Graciously Grant Us Peace

Cantata 42. Am Abend der desselbigen Sabaths
In The Evening Of The Same Sabbath

Nürnberg, 1531
Jos. Klug G. B., 1535

B. A. 10, 91

In gra-cious mer-cy grant us peace, O Lord, for life's du-ra-tion. We've none to help us should Thou cease to strive for our sal-va-tion. Thou art our sole Pro-tec-tor. In-sure us, through the ru-lers of our land, peace and good gov-ern-ment; That

un - der their com - mand, free from war and from tur-moil we may live and pros - per, up-right, pi - ous, re - ve - rent; Fear - ing the Lord. A - men.

Martin Luther, 1531 and 1566

323

Von Himmel hoch da komm ich her
From Heaven High Now Come I Here

Weihnachts-Oratorium
Christmas Oratorio

B. A. 5, II, 66

Val. Schumann G. B., 1539

Look, look, what mi - ra - cle is this? A
Be - hold, in gloom - y sta - ble stall, there

bea - con shines through night's a - byss. I
lies the Ru - ler of us all. Where

see a migh - ty
once the hun - gry

light a - far, which brigh - ter shines than brigh - test star.
ox - en fed, the Vir - gin finds her Child a - bed.

P. Gerhardt, 1666

324

Von Gott will ich nicht lassen
I Will Not Part From God

B. A. 39, Nº 164

Joach. Magdeburg, 1571

From God will no-thing part___ me, for by me He will
safe - est course will chart___ me, that I go not a-

stay; The stray. How-ev-er wide I roam, with

help - ing hand He leads___ me, at___ morn and___ eve - ning___

feeds___ me, though I be far___ from home.

Ludw. Helmbold, 1563 or '64

325

Von Gott wil ich nicht lassen
I Will Not Part From God

B. A. 39, N° 165

Joach. Magdeburg, 1571

From God I'll not be part - ed, nor will He part from me. My course by Him is__ chart - ed, a - cross life's storm - y sea. He reach - es out His hands, At morn and eve pro - tects__ me, and safe and sound di - rects me in__ far - off dis - tant lands.

Ludw. Helmbold, 1563 or '64

326

Von Gott will ich nicht lassen
I Will Not Part From God

B. A. 39, N° 166

Joach. Magdeburg, 1571

From God will no-thing part me, for by me He will
saf - est course will chart me, that I not go a

1.
stay. The

2.
stray. How - e - ver wide I roam, with

help - ing hand He leads me; At morn and eve - ning

feeds me, though I be far from home.

Ludw. Helmbold, 1563 or '64

327

Von Gott will ich nicht lassen
I Will Not Part From God

Unfinished Cantata: Lobt ihn mit Herz und Munde
Praise Him With Heart And Tongue

B. A. 41, 259

(Questionable authenticity)

Joach. Magdeburg, 1571

Praise God with hands and voi - ces, with heart and life and limb;

Cre - a - tion all re - joi - ces, each hour we think of Him.

While here on earth we live, our days and hours are wast -

ed, till bless-ed - ness we've tast - ed, that Hea- ven there will give.

Ludwig Helmbold, 1563 or '64

328

Von Gott will ich nicht lassen
I Will Not Part From God

Cantata 73. Herr, wie du willst

Lord, As Thou Wilt

B. A. 18, 104

Joach. Magdburg, 1571

It was our Fa-ther's plea - sure, that He cre - ate our
Son in full - est mea - sure, has shed on us His

race. His
Grace. The Ho - ly Ghost a - bove in

Hea - ven High is reign - ing, our laws and lives or -

dain - ing. To them be praise and love.

Ludw. Helmbold, 1563 or '64

329

Wachet auf, ruft uns die Stimme
Awaken, The Voice Calls To Us

Cantata 140. Wachet aus, ruft uns die Stimme
Awaken, The Voice Calls To Us (Sleepers, Awake)

Philipp Nicolai, 1599

B. A. 28, 284

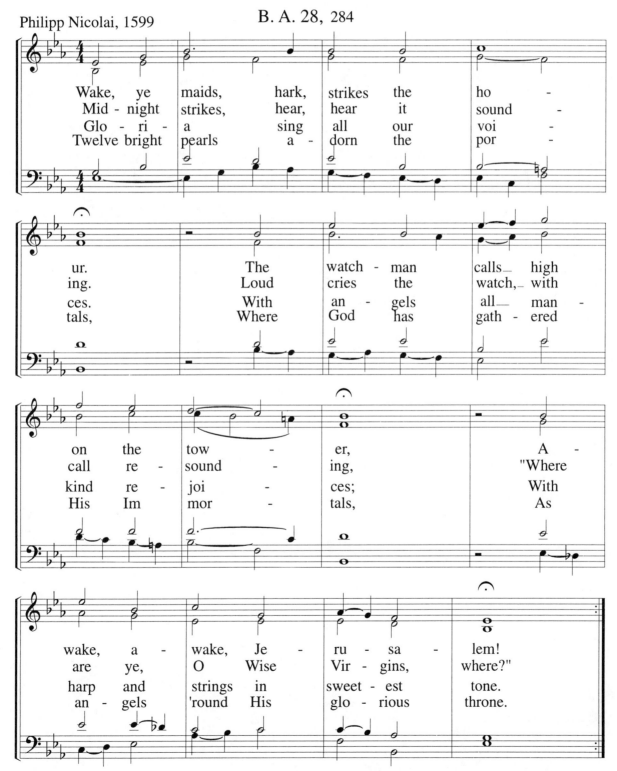

Good cheer, the Bride-groom comes. A -
No eye has ev - er seen,

rise and take your lamps! Al - le - lu -
ear has ev - er heard, The joy we

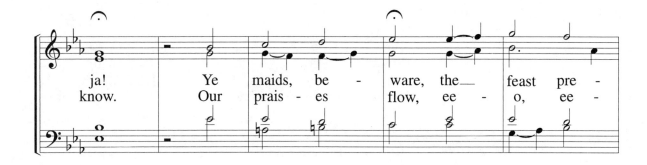

ja! Ye maids, be - ware, the feast pre -
know. Our prais - es flow, ee - o, ee -

pare, and go ye forth to meet Him there.
o, to God in dul - ci ju - bi - lo.

Philipp Nicolai, 1598

330

Wär' Gott nicht mit uns diese Zeit
Were God Not With Us Today

Cantata 14. Wär' Gott nicht mit uns
Were God Not With Us

B. A. 2, 132

Joh. Walther, 1524

Were God not with us here to-day, when foes do so as-
To God be praise and thanks that He, in dan-ger wat-ches

sail us, Faint-heart-ed, then we all would say: "Our cour-age now will
o'er us, And as a bird, from trap set free, to free-dom will re-

fail us." For we are but a fee-ble band, de-
store us. Re-leased from snare that held us there, His

spised and scorned on ev-'ry hand, with naught else to a-vail us.
Name is hon-ored ev-'ry where, by man and An-gel Cho-rus.

Martin Luther, 1524

331

Warum betrübst du dich, mein Herz
Why Art Thou Troubled, O My Heart

B. A. 39, N° 167

Barthol. Monœtius, 1565

Why art_ thou trou - bled, o my heart? So_ sore dis-tressed and

sad_ thou art. Why mourn earth's fleet - ing joys? Put_

thou thy trust in God, thy_ Lord, Cre - a - tor, He, by_ all a - dored.

Single sheet, Nürnberg, before 1565

332

Warum betrübst du dich, mein Herz
Why Art Thou Troubled, O My Heart

B. A. 39, N° 168

Barth. Moncetius, 1565

Single sheet, Nürnberg, before 1565

333

Warum betrübst du dich, mein Herz
Why Art Thou Troubled, O My Heart

Cantata 47. Wer sich selbst erhöhet
He Who Exalts Himself

B. A. 10, 274

Barth. Monœtius, 1565

All glo-ries of earth glad-ly I fore-go, if on-ly on me

Thou wilt be-stow, for-ev-er that re-ward, The

guer-don of Thy bit-ter woe: This ask I Thee, my God and Lord.

Single sheet, Nürnberg, before 1565

334

Warum sollt' ich mich denn grämen
Why Then Should I Grieve

B. A. 39, N° 169

J. G. Ebeling, 1666
D. Vetter, 1713

Why should sor - row so be-numb me? Thou art mine, I am Thine. Who can take Thee from me? Can I lose the Hea - ven won me by God's Son, By Him won, thus be-stowed up - on me?

P. Gerhardt, 1653

335

Warum sollt' ich mich denn grämen
Why Then Should I Grieve

Weihachts-Oratorium
Christmas Oratorio

J. G. Ebeling, 1666
D. Vetter, 1713

B. A. 5, 124

Joy - ful hearts are dan - cing, spring - ing, glad and gay, hap - py
Thee, my Mas - ter, faith - ful serv - ing, here live I. Here I

day. An - gels all are sing - ing. Hear their
die, die with faith un - swerv - ing. Then my

ring - ing tones so - no - rous: "Christ - mas morn,
soul, to Hea - ven soar - ing, soon will rise

Christ is born!" sings the An - gel Cho - rus.
through the skies, joy - ous and a - dor - ing.

P. Gerhardt, 1656

336

Was betrübst du dich, mein Herze
What Makes Thee Grieve, My Heart

B. A. 39, N° 170

Probably by J. S. Bach

What, my heart so dis - con - tents thee, Why so sor - row - ful art thou?

Tell me what it is tor - ments thee, Where is all thy cou - rage now?

What mis- for- tune brings thee sad- ness? Where has gone thy hope and glad-ness?

Where is thy con - tent- ment sweet, which through God was once com - plete?

Zacharias Hermann, around 1690

337

Was bist du doch, o Seele, so betrübet
Why Art Thou, My Soul, So Troubled

B. A. 39, N° 171

Freylinghausen G. B. 1702 (1703)

What is it, soul, that thus with woe af - fects thee?
Is it that God to bear a cross sub - jects thee?

What trou - bles thee so woe - ful-ly?

God loves thee still and as His own se - lects thee.

Rud. Fried. von Schult, before 1740

338

Was Gott thut, das ist wohlgethan
What God Does Is Well Done

Cantata 144. Nimm, was ist dein
Take What Is Thine

B. A. 30, 87

Nürnberg G. B., 1690

What | God does is with | rea - son done, of | this be ne'er for -
though at times our | joys are none, and | life is hard and

get - ful, Al - | fret - ful. He is thy guide, what - e'er be - tide, who

ev - er will up - hold thee, and in His i - mage mold thee.

Samuel Rodigast, 1675

339

Was Gott thut, das ist wohlgethan
What God Does Is Well Done

Trauungschoral

Wedding Chorale

B. A. 13 I, 147

Nürnberg G. B., 1690

Samuel Rodigast, 1675

340

Was Gott thut, das ist wohlgethan
What God Does Is Well Done

Cantata 12. Weinen, Klagen

Weep, Lament

B. A. 2, 78

Cantata 69. Lobe den Herrn, meine Seele

Praise The Lord, My Soul

B. A.16, 379

Nürnberg G. B., 1690

What God does is with rea-son done, this truth will not for-
though His will by thorn-y paths, through toil and trou-ble

sake me, Al - take me. My Fa - ther, He will care for me, se -

cure will He pro-tect me. Let Him a-lone di - rect me.

Samuel Rodigast, 1675

341

Was Gott thut, das ist wohlgethan
What God Does Is Well Done

Cantata 99. Was Gott thut, das ist wohlgethan

What God Does Is Well Done

B. A. 22, 276

Nürnberg G. B., 1690

What God does is with rea - son done; this truth will not_ for -
though His will by thorn - y path, through toil and trou - ble

1. sake me, Al -
2. take me. My Fa - ther, He will care for me, se -

cure will He_ pro - tect me. Let Him a - lone di - rect me.

Samuel Rodigast, 1675

380

342

Was mein Gott will, das g'scheh' allzeit
What My God Wills Always Comes to Pass

Matthäus-Passion
St. Matthew Passion

Joach. Magdeburg, 1572
(Original French melody)

B. A. 4, 53

What_ God re-solves will come a-bout, what He has done is_ fin-ished. He_
gives His help to all de-vout, whose faith is un-di- min-ished. Our

help in need,_our God in-deed, He tem-pers our cor-rec- tion with_ mer-cy just, So

Him we trust, se- cure in His af - fec - tion.

Albrecht, Margrave of Brandenburg-Culmbach, 1556

343

Was mein Gott will', das g'scheh' allzeit
What My God Wills Always Comes To Pass

Cantata 144. Nimm, was ist dein
Take What Is Thine

B. A. 30, 92

Joach. Magdeburg, 1572

What God re - solves will come a - bout, what He has done is
gives His help to all de - vout, whose faith is un - di -

1. fin - ished. He
2. min - ished. Our help in need, our God in -

,our help in need,

deed, He tem - pers our cor - rec - tion with mer - cy just, so

af - fec - tion.

Him we trust, as - sured of His af - fec - tion.

- sured of His af - fec - tion.

Albrecht, Margrave of Brandenburg-Culmbach, 1556

344

Was mein Gott will, das g'scheh' allzeit
What God Wills Always Comes To Pass

Cantata 72. Alles nur nach Gottes Willen

All By God's Will Alone

B. A. 18, 84

Joach. Magdeburg, 1572

What_ God re-solves will He a-chieve, His Will is per-fect
suc-cors all who firm be-lieve, and for the best en-

e - dea - ver. He_ vor. Our strength in need,_ our

God in-deed, with gen-tle mo-de-ra-tion He_

chas-tens us. If Him we trust, we need not fear dam-na-tion.

Albrecht, Margrave of Brandenburg-Culmbach, 1556

345

Was mein Gott will, das g'scheh' allzeit
What My God Wills Always Comes to Pass

Cantata 111. Was mein Gott will

What My God Wills

B. A. 24, 28

Joach. Magdeburg, 1572

Once more, O God, I ask of Thee, nor will Thou this de-
base temp- ta- tions trou- ble me, with Faith and Hope sup-

ny ____ me: When
ply ____ me. O God, our Lord, ____ Thy help af-

ford, Thy name to ren- der glo - rious; And send, I pray, that

Prom - ised Day, when right will be vic- to - rious.

Albrecht, Margrave of Brandenburg-Culmbach, 1656

384

346

Was mein Gott will, das g'scheh' allzeit
What My God Wills Always Comes To Pass

Cantata 65. Sie werden aus Saba alle kommen

You Shall All Come Out Of Sheba

B. A. 16, 166

Joach. Magdeburg, 1572

To God I give my heart and soul, and count it no____ pri - va -
so it seem, to me 'tis gain, for death is my____ sal - va -
If now, O Lord, it pleas-es Thee to take me in____ Thy keep -
tect Thou me and let this be, un - til in death____ I'm sleep -

1. & 3
tion. Though
ping. Pro -
2. & 4
tion. A son am I of God on
ing. My heart and soul do Thou con -

high, in Hea - ven High a - bove____ me. And_ though with
trol, they are of Thy cre - a - tion. So all my

woe my faith He try, yet ev - er He____ will love me.
days I sing thy praise in heart - felt a - do - ra - tion.

P. Gerhardt, 1648

385

347

Was mein Gott will, das g'scheh' allzeit
What My God Wills Always Comes To Pass

Cantata 92. Ich hab' in Gottes Herz und Sinn

I Have In God's Heart And Mind

B. A. 22, 68

Joach. Magdeburg, 1572

When I shall go the way from which no tra-vel-er
hope to find the heav'n-ly home for which my spi -

- re-turn eth, I eth. Thou art my Guide, what -
rit yearn -

e'er be-tide, what-ev-er may be-fall me, Un-til the day when

far a-way to Hea-ven Thou wilt call me.

P. Gerhardt, 1648

348

Was mein Gott will, das g'scheh' allzeit
What My God Wills Always Comes To Pass

Cantata 103. Ihr werdet weinen und heulen

You Shall Weep And Moan

B. A. 22, 68

Joach. Magdeburg, 1572

O— God of Mer - cy, do Thou heed Thy co - ve - nant to— mor — tals. Thou— por - tals, And I will— o - pen un - to thee, and grant to thee sal - va - tion, So— joy - ous thou wilt worship Me, in heart-felt a - do - ra - tion."

saidst: "Im-plore Me in thy need, and knock thou at my— hope of hap - pi - ness sub - lime, and bliss be - yond all trea - sure, The— mea - sure. I send re - lief— from trou - bles brief, by which you are sur - round - ed, And— on your head will rest in - stead the Crown of Joy un - bound - ed.

Though— I be gone a lit - tle time, my chil-dren, you may

1. & 3.

2. & 4.

P. Gerhardt, 1656

349

Was willst du dich, o meine Seele
What Dost Thou Want, O My Soul

B. A. 39, N° 172

Gottfried Vopelius, 1682

Why art thou, O my soul, for - ev - er griev - ing? Will not God care for thee, thy care re - liev - ing? Full well He knows how sore in need thou art; For grace and good - ness fills His ve - ry heart. With

pa - tience heed Him, How - e'er His will may lead Him. He can - not in thy bond-age now de - sert thee. Thou art His well-loved friend. Trust thou in God, on Him de - pend, dis - grace will ne - ver hurt thee.

? Dietr. von dem Werder, † 1657

350

Welt, ade! ich bin dein müde
World, Farewell! Of Thee I'm Weary

Cantata 27. Wer weiss, wie nahe mir mein Ende

Who Knows How Near To Me My End

B. A. 5 I, 244

Melody and harmonization by Johann Rosenmüller

Here on earth is strife and war, va - ni - ty and sore dis-tress,

There in Hea - ven ev - er - more,

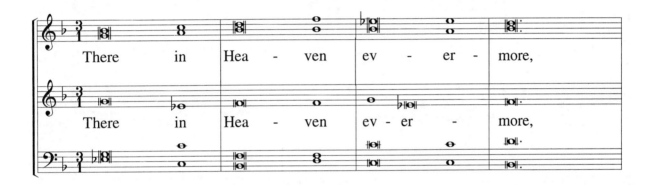

and Bless - ed - ness.

Peace and Rest and Bless - ed - ness.
and Bless - ed - ness.

Joh. G. Albinus, 1619

351

Weltlich Ehr' und zeitlich Gut
Wordly Fame And Earthly Gain

B. A. 39, N° 173

Vögelin G.B., 1563

World - ly fame and earth - ly gain, it's lust and ar - ro -
gant___ dis - dain is ev - en as the grass. Pride and
haugh - ti - ness will pass, Wi - ther as the mea - dow grass. Man, be -
think thee well of___ this, Lest thy life___ be led a - miss.
be led
be led
be led

Mich. Weisse, 1531

352

Wenn in Angst und Noth
When In Anguish And Need

B. A. 39, N° 174

M. A. v. Löwenstern, 1644

When grief my spi - rit fills, I lift un - to Thy hills mine eyes in pra - yer, Lord. Hear Thou my sup - pli - ca - tion, and turn Thine ear to me, that I go not from Thee, with sighs in de - so - la - tion.

M. A. v. Löwenstern, 1644

353

Wenn mein Stündlein vorhanden ist
When My Hour Is At Hand

B. A. 39, Nº 175

Church songs, Frankfurt on Main, 1569

When fi - nal - ly my ho - ur comes, and__ forth I must__ be

far - ing, let then Thy help, Lord__ Je - sus__ Christ, be__ nei - ther scant nor

spar - ing. My soul I place at__ Thy com-mand. Keep Thou it well with

lov - ing hand and to - le - rant for - bear - ing.

Nic. Herman, 1562

394

354

Wenn mein Stündlein vorhanden ist
When My Hour Is At Hand

B. A. 39, N° 176

Frankfurt on Main, 1589

When fi - nal - ly my ho - ur comes, and forth I must be

far - ing, let then Thy help, Lord Je - sus Christ, be nei - ther scant nor

spar - ing. My soul I place at Thy com - mand. Keep Thou it well with

lov - ing hand and to - le - rant for - bear - ing. for - bear - ing.

Nic. Herman, 1562

355

Wenn mein Stündlein vorhanden ist
When My Hour Is At Hand

B. A. 39, N° 177

Frankfurt on Main, 1569

When fi - nal - ly my ho - ur comes, and forth I must be far - ing, let then Thy help, Lord Je - sus Christ, be nei - ther scant nor spar - ing. My soul I place at Thy com - mand. Keep Thou it well, with lov - ing hand and to - le - rant for - bear - ing.

Nic. Herman, 1562

356

Wenn mein stündlein vorhanden ist
When My Hour Is At Hand

Cantata 95. Christus, der ist mein Leben

Christ, He Is My Life

B. A. 22, 153

Frankfurt on Main, 1569

Like Thee, the grave will not hold me for long in its sub-lec-tion. From death Thy Words have set me free, they are my re-sur-rec-tion. For where Thou art, there will I be, to live for-ev-er near to Thee; So forth I go re-joic-ing.

So forth I go re-joic-ing.

Nic. Herman, 1562

357

Wenn mein Stündlein vorhanden ist
When My Hour Is At Hand

Cantata 31. Der Himmel Lacht, die Erde jubiliret

Heaven Laughs, The Earth Jubilates

B. A. 7, 50

Frankfurt on Main G. B., 1569

With ea - ger, rea - dy arms out-streched, to— Je - sus I— be -
may I sleep in per - fect peace, no— mor - tal can a -

1.
take me. So

2.
wake me. For Je - sus is the—

on - ly— key that o - pens wide the Gates— for me, that

lead to Life E - ter - nal.
lead at last to a Life E - ter - nal.

lead to life E - ter - nal.

Nic. Herman, 1562

358

Wenn wir in höchsten Nöthen sein
When We Are In The Greatest Need

B. A. 39, N° 178

Franz Eler, 1588

Paul Eber, 1560

359

Wenn wir in höchsten Nöthen sein
When We Are In Greatest Need

B. A. 39, N°179

Franz Eler, 1588

When we are trou - bled through and through, and
art the com - fort, which a - lone, to

know not what we next may do; When
all Thy loy - al folk is known. Thou

help and coun - sel
faith - ful God, we

takes to flight, and cares op - press us day and night, Thou
cry to Thee, to save us from our

1.
mi - se - ry.
2.

Paul Eber, 1560

360

Werde munter, mein Gemüthe
Awaken, My Soul

Cantata 146. Wir müssen durch viel Trübsal

We Must, Through Much Affliction

B. A. 30, 190

Joh. Schop, 1642

Rouse thee up, my soul, from slum - ber, ea - ger go— thou
All the bless - ings with - out num - ber, God has here— con -

forth— and see
ferred— on thee.

How He guards us day by day;

drives our wea - ry cares— a - way;

How He loves us and be - friends us, safe from Sa - tan's— snares de - fends us.

Joh. Rist, 1642

361
Werde munter, mein Gemüthe
Awaken, My Soul

Matthäus-Passion

St. Matthew Passion

B. A. 4, 173

Joh. Schop, 1642

Though from Thee temp - ta - tion lured me, Lord, to Thee I
My for - giv - ness is as - sured me, thru Thy Son's de -

come a - gain. I do not_ de - ny my guilt;
spair and pain.

but Thy mer - cy,___ if Thou_ wilt, far ex - ceed - eth

all trans - gres - sion, of which I must_ make con - fes - sion.

Joh. Rist, 1642

402

362

Werde munter, mein Gemüthe
Awaken, My Soul

Cantata 55. Ich armer Mensch, ich Sündenknecht

I Poor Man, I Hardened Sinner

B. A. 12 II, 86

Joh. Schop, 1642

Though from Thee temp - ta - tion lured me, Lord, to Thee I
My for - giv - ness is as - sured me, thru Thy Son's de -

come a - gain. I do not de - ny my guilt;
spair and pain.

But Thy mer - cy, if Thou wilt, Far ex - ceed - eth

all trans - gres - sion, of which I must make con - fes - sion.

Joh. Rist, 1642

363

Werde munter, mein Gemüthe
Awaken, My Soul

B. A. 39, N° 106

Joh. Schop, 1642

Je - sus, Thou my soul's en - chant - ment,
Best de - light and Sun of Glad - ness,
Je - sus, my most pre - cious plea - sure,
Spi - rit's Pas - ture, choi - cest Trea - sure,

Thou who all my care dis - pel.
Je - sus whom I know so well,
Light of Faith and safe re - treat,
Help - er sure and Com - fort sweet.

Thee I love with all my heart. Sad the day if we should part.
O how longed for, O how dear, does Thy Name to me ap - pear.

Come Thou, Je - sus, come to me, bide with me e - ter - nal - ly.
To re - mem - ber what Thou art, makes to laugh my ach - ing heart.

Mart. Jahn, 1671

364

Werde munter, mein Gemüthe
Awaken, My Soul

B. A. 39, N° 107

Joh Schop, 1642

Je - sus, Thou my | soul's en - chant - ment, | Thou who all my
Best De - light and | Sun of Glad - ness, | Je - sus whom I

care dis - pel, | Thee I love with all my heart.
know so well.

Sad the day if we must____part. Come Thou, Je - sus,

come to me, bide with me e - ter - nal - ly.

Mart. Jahn, 1671

365

Werde munter, mein Gemüthe
Awaken, My Soul

Cantata 54. Mein liebster Jesu ist verloren

My Dearest Jesus Is Lost

B. A. 32, 65

Joh. Schop, 1642

Je - sus, Thou my / Blest Re - deem - er, / Je - sus, Safe Re -
Je - sus, Foe of / Foul Blas - phe - mer, / Je - sus, Bea - con

treat from strife, / How my heart will / joy - ous greet Thee.
of my Life!

How my spi - rit / yearns to meet Thee. / Come, o come, I

wait for Thee, / Come, my Je - sus, / dear to me!

Mart. Jahn (Janus), 1671

366
Wer Gott vertraut, hat wohlgebaut
Who Trusts In God Has Builded Well

B. A. 39, Nº 150

J. Magdeburg, 1572

S. Calvesius, 1597

Who trusts in God has build-ed well, on safe and
He who re - lies on Je - sus Christ, is cer-tain

sound foun-da - tion, on so - lid, sure foun - da - tion.
of sal - va - tion, yea, sure to gain sal - va - tion.

And so I place up - on Thy Grace my fast and

firm re - li - ance. When Thou art near, no harm I

fear, to death I bid de - fi - ance, to pain and death de - fi - ance.

Joach. Magdeburg, 1571

407

367

Wer nur den lieben Gott lässt walten
Who So Will Let Dear God Rule

B. A. 39, N° 180

Georg Neumark, 1640

Who - so will suf - fer God to guide___ him, and day by
won - drous al - ly has be - side___ him, when sore dis -

day in Him__ con - fide, A tide. He who with Migh - ty
tress and ill__ be__ -

God__ can stand, has build - ed on no__ shift - ing sand.

Georg Neumark,, 1640

368

Wer nur den lieben Gott lässt walten
Who So Will Let Dear God Rule

Cantata 88. Siehe, ich will viel Fischer aussenden

Behold, I Will Send Forth Many Fishes

B. A. 20 I, 178

Georg Neumark, 1640

Sing, pray and walk in God's own path - way, and do your
con - fi - dence in His rich bless - ing, will you, through

part with pur - pose true. By new. Who-so on God his
Him be born a -

faith has set, him ne - ver will his God for - get.

Georg Neumark, 1640

369

Wer nur den lieben Gott lässt walten
Who So Will Let Dear God Rule

Cantata 93. Wer nur den lieben Gott lässt walten

Whoso Will Let Dear God Rule

B. A. 22, 94

Georg Neumark, 1640

Sing, pray and walk in God's own path - way, and do your
con - fi - dence in His rich bless - ing, will you, through

part with pur - pose true. By
Him be born a -

new. Who - so on God his

faith has set, him ne - ver will his God for - get.

Georg Neumark, 1640

370

Wer nur den lieben Gott lässt walten
Who So Will Let Dear God Rule

Trauungscantate. Gott ist unser Zuversicht

Wedding Cantata. God Is Our Trust

B. A. 13 I, 144

Georg Neumark, 1640

So hap - py walk where God will lead you, and do your
thus may gain His grace and bless - ing, each morn-ing

part with pur - pose true. You new. Who-so on God his
gi - ven you a -

faith has set, him ne - ver will his God for - get.

Georg Neumark, 1640

371

Wer nur den lieben Gott lässt walten
Who So Will Let Dear God Rule

Cantata 179

Siehe zu, dass deine Gottesfurcht nicht Heuchelei sei

See To It That Thy Fear Of God Be Not Hypocrisy

B. A. 35, 292

Georg Neumark, 1640

A fee - ble soul, a fee - ble sin - ner, I stand be -
God, ah God, deal with me gent - ly; con-demn me

fore Thy Ma - jes - ty. Ah cree! Ah, pi - ty me, ah,
not by Thy de -

pi - ty me, Thou God of Mer - cy, pi - ty me.

Cristoph Tietze, 1663

372

Wer nur den lieben Gott lässt walten
Who So Will Let Dear God Rule

Cantata 166. Wo gehest du hin?

Whither Goest Thou?

B. A. 33, 122

Georg Neumark, 1640

Who knows how near is my last ho - ur? For there goes
how too sud - den - ly and swift - ly will come my

Time and here comes Death. Ah, breath. In Je - sus' Name I
fin - al dy - ing

ask of Thee, send Thou a gen - tle death to me.

Æmilia Juliana, Countess of Schwarzburg-Rudolstadt, 1688

413

373

Wer nur den lieben Gott lässt walten
Who So Will Let Dear God Rule

Cantata 84. Ich bin vergnügt mit meinem Glücke

I Take Delight In My Joy

B. A. 20 I, 98

Georg Neumark, 1640

And so I live in qui - et plea - sure, and
nit - ed with my God to trea - sure this

die in peace and free from grief; U -
stead - fast faith and

1. 2.

firm be - lief: "By

Grace, through what our Lord en - dured, my

soul's sal - va - tion is as - sured.

Æmilia Juliana, Countess of Schwarzburg-Rudolstadt, 1688

374

Wie bist du, Seele in mir so gar betrübt
Why Art Thou, My Soul, So Very Troubled

B. A. 39, Nº 182

Christian Brunmann (Mart. Hanke), 1675

How now, my spi - rit, why art so full of woe? Thy Sa - viour liv - eth, who tru - ly loves thee so. Do thou thine all to Him sur - ren - der, and feel His com - fort, kind and ten - der.

Tobias Zeutschner, 1667

375

Wie schön leuchtet der Morgenstern
How Beautifully Shines The Morning Star

B. A. 39, N° 183

Philipp Nicolai, 1599

How bright and fair the morn-ing star, the shin-ing mes - sen -
Son of Da-vid's roy - al line, be - lov - ed Lord and

ger a - far of Thine e - ter - nal bless - ing. Thou ses - ing.
Mas - ter mine, my heart and soul pos -

Kind - ly, friend - ly, fair and no - ble; Rich in boun - ty,

faith-less ne - ver; High en - throned a - bove for - e - ver.

Philipp Nicolai, 1599

376

Wie schön leuchtet der Morgenstern
How Beautifully Shines The Morning Star

Cantata 172. Erschallet, ihr Lieder

Resound, Ye Songs

B. A. 35, 69

Philipp Nicolai, 1599

O God,— when— Je - sus mine doth chance to cast on me a
Je - sus,— Thou who com - fort - eth, thy word, Thy Spi - rit,

kind - ly glance, Thy light of Joy in - spires me. O fires me.
life and death, with quick - ened cour - age

Take me, keep me, Thy pro - tec - tion, Thine af - fec - tion,

Love in still - ing. At Thy call I come all will - ing.

Philipp Nicolai, 1599

377

Wie schön leuchtet der Morgenstern
How Beautifully Shines The Morning Star

Cantata 36. Schwingt freudig euch empor

Joyously Ascend Upward

B. A. 7, 243

Philipp Nicolai, 1599

Strike strong the strings on lute and lyre, with harp and haut-boy,
Je - sus Christ the Lord is born; the joy - ful tid - ings,

song and choir, and hap-py voi - ces sing - ing; For ring - ing.
this bright morn, through all the world are

Hal - le - lu - jah! Sound your cym - bals, strike your tim - brels,

loud - er, fast - er!, Thank and glo - ri - fy our Mas - ter.

Philipp Nicolai, 159

418

378

Wie schön leuchtet der Morgenstern
How Beautifully Shines The Morning Star

Cantata 1. Wie schön leuchtet der Morgenstern

How Beautifully Shines The Morning Star

B. A. 1, 51

Philipp Nicolai, 1599

What joy my Sa-viour brings to me, my Al-pha and O-
dwell in Pa-ra-dise with Him, en-throned a-mong the

me-ga He, Be-gin-ning mine and end-ing; To scend-ing!
Se-ra phim, in bless-ed-ness tran-

A-men, A-men, Come, Thou fair-est Crown of Glad-ness,

wait no long-er; Thou for whom the world is yearn-ing!

Philipp Nicolai, 1599

379

Wir Christenleut'
We Christian People

Cantata 40. Dazu ist erschienen der Sohn Gottes

With This God's Son Is Come

B. A. 7, 377

Dresden G. B., 1593

Ye_ Chris - tians all! Ye Chris - tians all, with
Sin_ brings but grief. It brings but grief, but

joy re - call how Christ be - came a man of low - ly
true be - lief, be - lief in Christ, brings joy and sure sal -

sta - tion. They who be - lieve, will God re - ceive in
va - tion. When God is near, we need not fear that

Hea - ven with the An - gel Con - gre - ga - tion.
an - y Chris - tian soul en - dure dam - na - tion.

Caspar Füger, about 1552

380

Wir Christenleut'
We Christian People

Cantata 110. Unser Mund sei voll Lachen

Let Our Mouth Be Full Of Laughter

B. A. 23, 324

Dresden G. B., 1593

Al - le - lu - ja! Give praise to God. In song to - ge - ther join in deep e - mo - tion, For God to - day has brought such joy, that ev - 'ry hour in - crea - ses our de - vo - tion.

Caspar Füger, about 1552

381

Wir Christenleut'
We Christian People

Weihnachts-Oratorium

Christmas Oratorio

B. A. 5, 126

Dresden G. B., 1593

Re - joice and sing, re - joice and sing, your

Heav'n - ly King, as man is born, and lays a - side His

glo - ry. He is a - dored as Christ the Lord, and

ev' - 'ry tongue re - peats His won - drous sto - ry.

382

Wir glauben all' an einen Gott
We All Believe In One God

B. A. 39, Nº 184

Joh. Walther G. B., 1524

flour - ish. From mis-hap will He de-fend us. No harm ev - er can at-tend us. He cares for us all, guards us well, our migh-ty fort and ci - ta - del.

Martin Luther, 1524

383

Wo Gott der Herr nicht bei uns hält
Were God The Lord Not On Our Side

B. A. 39, N° 6

Jos. Klug, 1535

Were God the Lord not on our side when
He no longer be our guide through

foes so strong assail us; Should ail us; Did
all the ills that

He remain aloof above, deny to us His

care and love, ah then all hope would fail us.

Justus Jonas, 1524

425

384

Wo Gott der Herr nicht bei uns hält
Were God The Lord Not On Our Side

Cantata 178. Wo Gott der Herr nicht bei uns hält
Were God The Lord Not On Our Side

B. A. 35, 272

Jos. Klug G. B., 1535

Lord God, we thank Thee ev'ry hour for all Thy precious
This foil our foes is in Thy pow'r, support us lest we
earth below and Heav'n above hast Thou, Lord God, cre-
by the radiance of Thy love, our hearts illumi-

1. favor. To
a - ted. And

2. waver. When
na - ted. Though

Faith and Reason must succumb, with no belief in
men may scoff, our Faith in Thee unfaltering will

things to come, how may we cease to qua - ver?
ev - er be, our fer - vor un - a - ba - ted.

Justus Jonas, 1524

385

Wo Gott der Herr nicht bei uns hält
Were God The Lord Not On Our Side

B. A. 39, 4

Jos. Klug G. B., 1535

Keep up your cou - rage Chris - tian folk, Why
was the Lord im - posed this yoke, So

are ye thus de - spair - ing? It
bear it brave, de -

clar - ing: "This

pun - ish - ment de - serve we all, on each we reck - on

it must fall; A - like we all are far - ing."

Joh. Gigas (Heune), 1561

427

386

Wo Gott der Herr nicht bei uns hält
Were God The Lord Not On Our Side

Cantata 114. Ach lieben Christen, seid getrost

Ah Dear Christians, Be Comforted

B. A. 24, 108

Jos. Klug G. B., 1535

When we a - wake or when we sleep, the
be bap - tised in Him will keep our

Lord is our good Pas - tor. To
souls from Hell's dis -

1. as - ter. All

e - vil sprang from A - dam's Fall, but Christ's A - tone - ment

saved us all; So praise our Lord and Mas - ter.

Joh. Gigas (Heune), 1561

387

Wo Gott der Herr nicht bei uns hält
Were God The Lord Not On Our Side

Cantata: Siehe, es hat überwunden der Löwe

Behold, The Lion Has Overcome

B. A. 41, 258

Jos. Klug G. B., 1535

Questionable authenticty

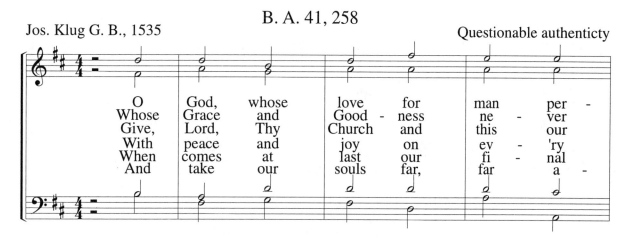

O God, whose love for man per -
Whose Grace and Good - ness ne - ver
Give, Lord, Thy and Church joy on this our
With peace and joy last our ev - 'ry
When comes at our souls far, fi - nal

vades Thy ve - ry
fades, and knows no
land, Thine A - gels
hand, good - will and
day, from Sa - tan's
way, to A - bram's

heart's foun - da - tion,
li - mi ta - tion.
for pro - tec - tion.
Thine af - fec - tion.
pow - er spare us.
bo - som bear us.

429

We thank Thee, Lord, for
The De - vil's mur - d'rous
That all the world with

Thou art true, Thy
guile, O Lord, his
prai - ses ring, as

bless - ings come each morn - ing
god less realm and hell - ish
Ho - ly, Ho - ly, Ho - ly

new, through all our
horde bring the Thou to
sing the An - gels

life's du - ra - tion.
swift de - struc - tion.
ne - ver ceas - ing.

Justus Gesenius, 1646

388

Wo Gott der Herr nicht bei uns hält
Were God The Lord Not On Our Side

B. A. 39, N° 5

Jos. Klug G. B., 1535

Were God not with us here to-day, when
heart-ed then we all would say: "Our

trou-bles do as-sail us, Faint fail us." For
cou-rage now doth

we are but a fee-ble band, de-spised and scorned on

ev-'ry hand, with naught else to a-vail us.

Martin Luther, 1524

389

Wo Gott zum Haus nicht gibt sein' Gunst
The House That God Does Not Protect

Psalm 127

B. A. 39, Nº 185

Jos. Klug G. B., 1535

? Johann Kolross, 1525